Countering Russia

The Role of Special Operations Forces in Strategic Competition

STEPHEN WATTS, SEAN M. ZEIGLER, KIMBERLY JACKSON,
CAITLIN MCCULLOCH, JOSEPH CHERAVITCH, MARTA KEPE

T0308575

Prepared for the United States Army
Approved for public release; distribution unlimited

RAND
CORPORATION

For more information on this publication, visit **www.rand.org/t/RRA412-1**.

About RAND

Research Integrity

Published by the RAND Corporation, Santa Monica, Calif.

Library of Congress Cataloging-in-Publication Data is available for this publication.

ISBN: 978-1-9774-0730-6

Cover: U.S. Marine Corps photo by Lance Cpl. Clare Shaffer.

Limited Print and Electronic Distribution Rights

Preface

This report documents research and analysis conducted as part of a project entitled *Leveraging Operational and Strategic Maneuver to Counter Revisionist States*, sponsored by the U.S. Army Special Operations Command. The purpose of the project was to establish a strategic framework for U.S. Army special operations forces to support countering Russian activities in the competition space.

This research was conducted within RAND Arroyo Center's Strategy, Doctrine, and Resources Program. RAND Arroyo Center, part of the RAND Corporation, is a federally funded research and development center (FFRDC) sponsored by the United States Army.

RAND operates under a "Federal-Wide Assurance" (FWA00003425) and complies with the *Code of Federal Regulations for the Protection of Human Subjects Under United States Law* (45 CFR 46), also known as "the Common Rule," as well as with the implementation guidance set forth in DoD Instruction 3216.02. As applicable, this compliance includes reviews and approvals by RAND's Institutional Review Board (the Human Subjects Protection Committee) and by the U.S. Army. The views of sources utilized in this study are solely their own and do not represent the official policy or position of DoD or the U.S. Government.

Contents

Figures, Tables, and Boxes

Figures

Tables

Boxes

Summary

Although U.S. strategic guidance proclaims that the United States has entered a new era of great-power competition, concepts for succeeding in that competition remain underdeveloped. This report focuses on the role of U.S. Army special operations forces (ARSOF) in competition. It addresses three questions:

- What sorts of activities is the United States likely to need to conduct in competition with Russia?
- Among these activities, what are ARSOF's areas of comparative advantage?
- What evidence exists on the effectiveness of the types of activities ARSOF conducts?

We analyzed requirements for competition through (1) a review of official guidance, military doctrine, and the broader policy literature in this field and (2) interviews with members of the special operations community and officials throughout the U.S. government. We analyzed ARSOF's effectiveness in addressing these competition requirements through a review of quantitative evidence and select case studies focused on Russia (and, previously, the Soviet Union).

Findings

The literature review and interviews conducted for this project suggest a broad range of requirements for the United States to compete successfully with Russia and other great powers, including the capability to mitigate adversarial messaging efforts, engage key populations, support decisionmakers against influence efforts by malign actors, improve the resilience of partner institutions, assure foreign partners of U.S. resolve, deter adversaries, and illuminate and disrupt adversary networks. ARSOF can make important contributions in all these areas.

Under steady-state conditions, ARSOF can help to strengthen the resilience of allies and partners while improving the United States' situational awareness. ARSOF activities may also send a deterrent signal to adversaries, although the evidence of such outcomes is less clear.

In conditions of more intensified competition, when the risk of armed conflict is high, ARSOF can help to defend against proxy forces used by U.S. adversaries. ARSOF can also be used to disrupt adversary operations in denied environments or to impose costs on adversaries, although the most aggressive uses of ARSOF—unconventional warfare intended to overthrow adversary governments—have traditionally been high-risk activities with relatively low rates of success.

ARSOF can also be used to better target U.S. operations in the information environment and work with local surrogates to strengthen the impact of such efforts.

Table S.1 provides a summary of potential U.S. goals in competition and the advantages and limitations of ARSOF in achieving them.

Policy Recommendations

The report offers the following recommendations to maximize the impact of ARSOF:

- The U.S. Army should revise future iterations of its multi-domain operations (MDO) concept and other formal publications to provide more-concrete guidance for competition and the employment of ARSOF.
- In cooperation with U.S. Special Operations Command, the Office of the Assistant Secretary of Defense for Special Operations and Low-Intensity Conflict, and other key stakeholders in the U.S. government, U.S. Army Special Operations Com-

Table S.1
Summary of ARSOF Strengths and Limitations in Strategic Competition

Potential U.S. Goals	ARSOF Strengths	ARSOF Risks and Limitations
• Mitigate adversarial messaging efforts • Engage key populations • Support decisionmakers against influence efforts by malign actors • Improve resilience of partner institutions • Assure foreign partners of U.S. resolve • Deter adversaries • Illuminate and disrupt adversary networks	• Ability to enhance partners' capabilities (for internal resilience and external deterrence) through low cost, persistent presence • Capabilities for low-visibility roles, including in tracking adversary activity and preparations for higher-intensity contingencies • Ability to effectively counter violent activities by surrogates • Ability to disrupt adversary networks in contested environments • Some ability to threaten adversary governments through unconventional warfare • Ability to enhance effectiveness of OIE through on-the-ground message targeting and recruitment of surrogates	• Challenges in developing sustainable capabilities in partners with poor political, economic development • Risk of misuse of capabilities developed in partners • Limitations in deterrent signal of ARSOF • High risk of failure when directly targeting adversary governments through UW (outside of foreign occupations) • Overall impact of OIE highly contingent on circumstances

mand should periodically review allocations of ARSOF against the evidence of utility in strategic competition to ensure optimal employment.

- Given the high levels of risk and the other instruments available to it, the U.S. government should use ARSOF for cost-imposing strategies only in relatively rare circumstances.
- Because the gains achieved through special operations tend to be incremental and are realized through local partners with their own objectives, it is imperative that the U.S. government embed special operations in a broader, long-term political-military strategy.

Acknowledgments

We thank U.S. Army Special Operations Command for sponsoring the research that led to this report, facilitating clearances and meetings, and providing valuable feedback throughout the process. We are grateful to Robert Warburg and Larry Deel for overseeing the research and to Robert Toguchi and Joseph Brecher for their input and suggestions. We are particularly grateful to Brooke Tannehill, who was an invaluable facilitator of our work throughout the year we spent working on this report.

The role of U.S. Army special operations forces in competition with other great powers is often clouded in secrecy. It is possible to engage in important strategic debates without recourse to classified information, but much of the necessary knowledge can be gained only by talking extensively to professionals in this field. Consequently, we are highly indebted to the many special operations forces personnel and others who took the time to speak with us in the course of our research. We promised to use all information gained from these interviews on a not-for-attribution basis, so we cannot thank everyone who helped us by name. We can, however, thank a handful of people who helped to arrange meetings for us. We are grateful for the assistance of NATO Special Operations Headquarters (especially Vice Admiral Colin Kilrain and Steven Mirr), U.S. Special Operations Command Central (especially Rear Admiral Wyman Howard and Lieutenant Colonel Catherine Crombe), and staff from the Office of the Secretary of Defense, the Joint Staff, U.S. European Command, U.S. Special Operations Command Europe, and the U.S. State Department. We are also grateful to a number of retired officers and other U.S. government employees who helped us understand special operations and interagency processes, including Lieutenant General (retired) Charles Cleveland, Javed Ali, and Christopher Costa.

Finally, we thank the reviewers of this report—Christopher Paul of RAND and Jonathan Schroden of CNA—for their valuable comments and suggestions.

Abbreviations

3ie	International Initiative for Impact Evaluation
ACD	Armed Conflict Dataset
ARSOF	U.S. Army special operations forces
BPC	building partner capacity
CAO	civil affairs operations
CENTCOM	U.S. Central Command
CIA	Central Intelligence Agency
CTS	Iraqi Counter Terrorism Service
DHS	U.S. Department of Homeland Security
DoD	U.S. Department of Defense
ESAF	El Salvador Armed Forces
FBI	Federal Bureau of Investigation
FID	foreign internal defense
FMLN	Farabundo Martí National Liberation Front
IE	information environment
IO	information operations
ISIL	Islamic State of Iraq and the Levant

MDO	multi-domain operations
MISO	military information support operations
NATO	North Atlantic Treaty Organization
NDS	National Defense Strategy
NSA	Non-State Actor dataset
NSS	National Security Strategy
OIE	operations in the information environment
PSYOP	psychological operations
SFA	Security Force Assistance
SFAB	security force assistance brigade
SOCCENT	U.S. Special Operations Command Central
SOCEUR	U.S. Special Operations Command Europe
SOF	special operations forces
UCDP-PRIO	Uppsala Conflict Data Program–Peace Research Institute Oslo
USAID	U.S. Agency for International Development
USASOC	U.S. States Army Special Operations Command
USSOCOM	U.S. Special Operations Command
USSR	Union of Soviet Socialist Republics
UW	unconventional warfare
VSO	Vetted Syrian Opposition (group)

CHAPTER ONE

Introduction

The U.S. defense community has decisively reoriented from the counterterrorism missions that dominated its focus for more than a decade toward a renewed focus on competition with near-peer adversaries. According to the current *U.S. National Security Strategy* (NSS) and *National Defense Strategy* (NDS), "Long-term strategic competitions with China and Russia are the principal priorities" for the U.S. Department of Defense (DoD). Moreover, these and other "actors have become skilled at operating below the threshold of military conflict."[1] What exactly is involved in this "competition," however, is unclear, as is which military tools can contribute to setting more favorable terms for competition.

This report examines one key set of U.S. military tools for competition—U.S. Army special operations forces (ARSOF)—and how they might be used to counter various threats in the competition space and seize competitive advantage. The focus of this report is on Russia, although many of our findings may be more broadly applicable to what the NSS refers to as "revisionist states." More specifically, this report addresses three questions:

- What sorts of activities is the United States likely to need to conduct to defend its interests and gain competitive advantage?

---

[1] The White House, *National Security Strategy of the United States of America*, Washington, D.C., December 2017, p. 3; U.S. Department of Defense, *Summary of the National Defense Strategy of the United States of America: Sharpening the American Military's Competitive Edge*, Washington, D.C., 2018, p. 4.

- Among these activities, what are ARSOF's areas of comparative advantage or disadvantage vis-à-vis conventional forces and other government agencies?
- What evidence exists on the effectiveness of the types of activities ARSOF conducts?

We draw on what we learned from investigating these questions to make recommendations for how the value of ARSOF can be best realized in strategic competition and ways in which these forces can be better integrated into the Army's and DoD's future thinking on competition. This report will likely be of primary interest to military planners focused on strategic competition, but it also has implications for the national security community more broadly.

Background: Gaps in Military Concepts for Competition

Fighting and winning wars against near-peer competitors, though extraordinarily complex, is an undertaking that the DoD is well suited to pursue. Operating below the threshold of military conflict, on the other hand, involves many activities at which DoD, as a whole, is less adept. The NDS seems to recognize the need to shift DoD's traditional way of thinking when it implores leaders to "foster a competitive mindset."[2] But the NDS does not articulate what such a mindset might entail. Later efforts to provide more-concrete concepts for competition, such as the Joint Doctrine Note on the "Competition Continuum," are similarly vague.[3]

The Army's concept for multi-domain operations (MDO) takes important steps toward detailing what DoD and the Army specifically can contribute to great-power competition. It establishes competition as a phase of equal importance to conflict and defines central elements of the military's role in competition, including (1) enabling the defeat

---

[2] U.S. Department of Defense, 2018, p. 5.

[3] Joint Chiefs of Staff, *Competition Continuum*, Washington, D.C., Joint Doctrine Note 1-19, June 3, 2019.

of information warfare and unconventional warfare (UW), (2) conducting intelligence and counter-reconnaissance, and (3) demonstrating a credible deterrent.[4] Despite these advances, the pamphlet outlining the Army's MDO concept gives greater emphasis to the Army's role in armed conflict than to competition,[5] and, in discussing information warfare, fails to provide a full treatment of the complex ways in which the United States military might be used to combat the concerted (mis) information campaigns of its adversaries.

Perhaps most surprising are the limited discussions in all these documents of the use of ARSOF in strategic competition. Long before ARSOF were used for counterterrorism missions, these forces were created for combat and competition with other great powers. Many of the U.S. antecedents of contemporary ARSOF arose in response to the exigencies of World War II, and they provided perhaps the preeminent military tools for competition with the Soviet Union in the Cold War.[6]

The broader policy literature on special operations provides more detail on ways in which ARSOF might be used in competition, detailing the ways in which ARSOF can be used to enhance conventional deterrence by developing territorial self-defense forces, combat information warfare through psychological operations and civil affairs personnel, impose costs on aggressors through unconventional warfare, and enhance allies' and partners' capabilities for resisting the malign acts of countries like Russia.[7] However, this literature lacks much of

---

4 U.S. Army Training and Doctrine Command (TRADOC), *The U.S. Army in Multi-Domain Operations 2028*, Fort Eustis, Va., TRADOC Pamphlet 525-3-1, December 6, 2018.

5 TRADOC, 2018, Chapter 3.

6 See, for instance, David Tucker and Christopher J. Lamb, *United States Special Operations Forces*, New York: Columbia University Press, 2007, Chapter 3.

7 See for instance Joseph L. Votel, Charles T. Cleveland, Charles T. Connett, and Will Irwin, "Unconventional Warfare in the Gray Zone," *Joint Force Quarterly*, Vol. 80, 1st Quarter 2016; ADM (R) Eric Olson [former SOCOM commander], "America's Not Ready for Today's Gray Wars," *Defense One*, December 10, 2015; Robert Haddick, *How Do SOF Contribute to Comprehensive Deterrence?* MacDill Air Force Base, Fla.: Joint Special Operations University Press, JSOU Report 17-11 2017; Chad M. Pillai, "The Dark Arts: Application of Special Operations in Joint Strategic and Operational Plans," *Small Wars Journal*, June 7, 2018.

the information that decisionmakers would want to understand before committing to using ARSOF in new or unfamiliar ways. Much of this vagueness is understandable: Special operations are often classified and challenging to observe, and by design they tend to avoid publicity. Nonetheless, it is extremely important to ground public debates about the strategic utility of ARSOF on rigorous analysis.

This report seeks to address these gaps by providing a high-level overview of requirements for strategic competition with Russia and the full range of ways in which ARSOF could improve the U.S. position in this competition. The report provides a framework for understanding potential contributions of ARSOF to great-power competition, an analysis of the effectiveness of a range of special operations in varying contexts, and an assessment of the limits of what ARSOF can realistically accomplish.

Research Scope and Approach

Research Scope and Definitions

Before detailing the research involved in this study, it is important to set out key definitions and describe the scope of this report.

U.S. Army Special Operations Forces

The focus of this report is on ARSOF, including Special Forces, psychological operations (PSYOP), and civil affairs. ARSOF are the largest of the four services' special operations components, and they are expert in many of the special operations forces (SOF) community's key capabilities for competition.

Russia and Revisionist States

The NSS singles out two categories of states that the United States prioritizes in strategic competition: the two "revisionist states" of China and Russia and the two "rogue states" of Iran and North Korea. The NSS never defines the concept of revisionism, but it is a term used widely in the field of international relations to refer to states that "seek to increase, not just keep, their resources. [Such states] often share a common desire to overturn the status quo order—the prestige, resources, and principles of the system."[8] Because of Russia's frequent use as a "pacing threat" for the Army and its frequent employment of malign activities short of armed conflict with the United States, the focus of this report is on Russia.[9]

Competitive Environments

As defined in DoD documents, the competition space is extremely broad, covering nearly all activities short of direct military conflict in which any element of coercion is present.[10] A wide range of military capabilities is relevant to the concept of competition, from conventional deterrence to instruments for combating nonconventional or irregular threats, including political subversion and proxy warfare. In this report, we focus on a wide range of ARSOF capabilities relevant to the nonconventional or irregular aspects of competition, including foreign internal defense (FID), UW, operations in the information environment (OIE), and general security cooperation and presence activities.

Because the competition space is so broad, we sometimes distinguish in this report between three broad contexts: steady-state environments, intensified environments, and the information environment. Steady-state and intensified competitive environments are both depicted in Figure 1.1, while the information environment pervades all the other environments.

Figure 1.1
Competition and Conflict Continuum

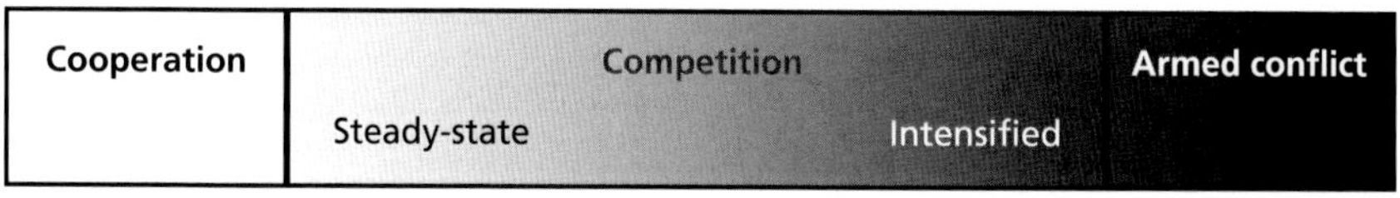

[8] Randall L. Schweller, "Tripolarity and the Second World War," *International Studies Quarterly*, Vol. 37, No. 1, 1993, p. 76.

[9] Some findings may be relevant to strategic competition with other actors, but a detailed analysis of these other contexts was beyond the scope of this study.

[10] Joint Chiefs of Staff, 2019.

Steady-state competitive environments are typical of the conduct of strategic competition. In these environments, actors seek to protect and advance their own interests without approaching the level of armed conflict. These environments are distinguished from purely cooperative environments in that the United States is actively trying to diminish the influence of other actors. Steady-state competitive environments are distinguished from intensified environments in the degree of risk of armed conflict—and the degree of risk U.S. decisionmakers are likely to accept when employing ARSOF. Steady-state activities aim to influence and shape conditions so they are favorable to the interest of the United States and its partners and to counter similar efforts conducted by the United States' adversaries. Security cooperation activities are one of the most commonly employed tools of competition in this environment. For example, U.S. military units might maintain an ongoing relationship with a partner-nation force, or an ARSOF unit might help a guerrilla force develop capabilities and infrastructure in anticipation of eventual escalation to an intensified situation.

We use the term *intensified environments* to describe situations that have escalated further than steady-state but have not yet breached the threshold of active armed conflict between the United States and its strategic competitor (although armed conflict, such as proxy wars, may have erupted in the countries in which that competition takes place). Although this term is not formally used in U.S. government publications, we selected it to capture the range of stages in competition that are not easily defined and are most applicable to the scope of this report. Many writings refer to this environment as the "gray zone" just below armed conflict.

As competition escalates, a range of tools become relevant that are unlikely to be used during ordinary steady-state conditions because of risk to U.S. military personnel, operational risk, or other concerns. These tools include many of the core competencies of ARSOF:

- In an intensified environment, and particularly with regard to countering revisionist states, UW can be used to develop and enable a resistance force capable of fighting a potential foreign occupying force. UW can also be conducted in an intensified environment if U.S. policy goals are to disrupt or replace the nation's existing government.

- FID in an intensified environment can be quite broad. Three categories of FID exist: indirect support, noncombat direct support, and U.S. combat operations, where U.S. and host-nation forces either conduct combined or integrated operations, or U.S. forces operate in place of host-nation forces. One specific subset of activities ARSOF might undertake in intensified settings is described as *preparation of the environment*, which is utilized "for developing and preparing for the entry of forces and supporting agencies to resolve conflicts using either lethal or nonlethal actions."[11] Per Joint Publication 1-02, *preparation of the environment* is "an umbrella term for operations and activities conducted by selectively trained special operations forces to develop an environment for potential future special operations."[12] In other words, although preparation of the environment is not a lethal activity in and of itself, it can be conducted in intensified environments to better understand key characteristics of a specific region, population, or both that would be critical for U.S. or friendly forces to know in the event of a future, more active conflict.

Finally, we distinguish the information environment from both steady-state and intensified environments. According to the *Joint Concept on Operations in the Information Environment*, the information environment (IE) may be defined as the aggregate of

> numerous social, cultural, cognitive, technical, and physical attributes that act upon and impact knowledge, understanding, beliefs, world views, and, ultimately, actions of an individual, group, system, community, or organization. The IE also includes

---

[11] Joint Chiefs of Staff, *Special Operations*, Washington, D.C., Joint Publication 3-05, 2011, p. II-5.

[12] Joint Chiefs of Staff, *Department of Defense Dictionary of Military and Associated Terms*, Washington, D.C., Joint Publication 1-02, February 15, 2016, p. 187.

> technical systems and their use of data. The IE directly affects and transcends all [operating environments].[13]

As this definition makes clear, the information environment influences the conduct and outcomes of all U.S. operations in both steady-state and intensified competitive environments.

Research Approach

There were four main steps in our research.

The first step was to review the existing literature, both official and unofficial, to understand how relevant stakeholders understand the role of ARSOF in great-power competition. We reviewed official strategic guidance documents; military doctrine, concepts, policies, and strategies; concepts and white papers for the employment of ARSOF; and articles, reports, and papers from think tanks, military schoolhouses, professional military journals, and policy journals and blogs.

The second step was to develop a greater understanding of ARSOF's capabilities and potential and especially its advantages and limitations relative to other instruments of the U.S. government. We reviewed special operations doctrine, concepts, and policies; histories of special operations; and secondary literature from this policy realm, and we conducted numerous interviews with personnel from the U.S. Department of State, the Office of the Secretary of Defense, the Joint Staff, two Theater Special Operations Component Commands, U.S. Army Special Operations Command (USASOC), the Naval Special Warfare Center, NATO Special Operations Headquarters, and forward-deployed personnel. These interviews included personnel from the United States and from European allies, civilians and military personnel, and personnel from multiple services' SOF. Information from these sources was then synthesized by research team members with years of experience working in relevant fields.

The third step consisted of a review of and, in some cases, extension of quantitative analyses of the effectiveness of operations in rel-

---

[13] Joint Chiefs of Staff, *Joint Concept for Operating in the Information Environment*, Washington, D.C., July 25, 2018.

evant fields. Because of data limitations, we were seldom able to conduct quantitative analyses of special operations themselves. Instead, we made use of broader analyses of the effectiveness of security sector assistance, deterrence, FID conducted in ongoing conflicts, covert attempts at regime overthrow, and a wide range of public communications campaigns.[14] Table 1.1 summarizes the type of operation or activity we analyzed; the state of existing, publicly available analysis; and how we adapted these existing studies for our project.

In our discussion of these studies in this report, we note where the results pertain specifically to ARSOF. In studies not specifically focused on ARSOF, we discuss the reasons why we believe inferences can be made from these studies, as well as caveats or limitations on the analysis when applied to ARSOF.

In a fourth step, we conducted case studies relevant to the use of SOF in competition with Russia. We report briefly on six cases:

- Building UW capacity in the Baltics, 2014–2019

Table 1.1
Summary of Research Approach for Analyses of Effectiveness

Type of Activity or Operation	Status of Existing Rigorous Analysis	Adaptation
Security cooperation	Limited number of directly relevant, rigorous studies	Literature review
FID	Very limited number of directly relevant, rigorous studies	Extensions of prior RAND analysis
UW	Very limited number of directly relevant, rigorous studies	Extensions on existing statistical analysis
OIE	Several dozen studies in fields related to OIE	Systematic literature review

[14] *Covert action*, defined in U.S. Code, refers to activities in which the actor's identity will not be publicly acknowledged. U.S. covert action requires a presidential finding. *Clandestine* activities, undefined in statute, describe when the operation itself is intended to be concealed, rather than the actor conducting them (Michael DeVine, *Covert Action and Clandestine Activities of the Intelligence Community: Selected Definitions in Brief*, Washington, D.C.: Congressional Research Service, June 14, 2019).

- The Iraqi Counterterrorism Service, 2003–2019
- Support to El Salvador, 1980–1992
- Operations at the Al-Tanf Garrison, 2017–2019
- Poland's Solidarity movement and covert U.S. OIE, 1980s
- U.S. OIE in the Balkans, 1992–2017.

The results of these case studies further inform our assessments of the effectiveness of ARSOF, providing nuance to the high-level but more abstract findings derived from statistical analyses.

Organization of This Report

The remainder of this report consists of three chapters. In Chapter Two, we provide a brief overview of the irregular threats the United States faces in competition with Russia and describe ARSOF capabilities for competition below armed conflict. We then discuss advantages and disadvantages of potential activities led by ARSOF, as well as advantages and disadvantages of potential activities led by conventional forces and/or other U.S. government agencies. In Chapter Three, we discuss what we learned about the effectiveness of the types of operations ARSOF could conduct in the competitive space, focusing in particular on security cooperation, FID, UW, and OIE. In Chapter Four, we highlight our conclusions and offer recommendations for how ARSOF may best be used to pursue U.S. goals in strategic competition with Russia. The appendix provides a technical discussion of statistical modeling of FID.

CHAPTER TWO

ARSOF Capabilities for Strategic Competition

The competition space between the United States and Russia is broad, encompassing a spectrum of military activities. ARSOF are deployed in many areas around the world, but the majority of these activities occur in areas where the threat of active conflict with U.S. forces is low and engagements are not intended to facilitate a direct, near-term U.S. role in military operations. These can include largely peacetime activities, whose aims are to strengthen relationships, build partner capabilities, assure partners and deter potential adversaries, and increase U.S. forces' awareness and familiarity of these non-hostile environments.

Areas where ARSOF are employed can also be characterized by increased hostilities. They can include countries at a higher risk of descending into violence and others that have already descended into irregular conflict (such as civil wars, often with great-power support to proxies on either side). Such environments are still generally considered to be short of conflict environments, as captured in the Army's MDO concept, with its focus on high-end, conventional warfare.

Throughout these competitive environments, ARSOF can play a major role, in some cases through security cooperation authorities and in other cases through operational authorities.

Background

Competitive activities that ARSOF can undertake include security cooperation and other engagements that serve to strengthen relationships—such as trainings that benefit all participants, subject-matter-expert exchanges, efforts to establish and clarify intelligence-sharing agreements, and a physical presence that might help assure U.S. partners and potentially help to deter adversaries—as well as core SOF activities of UW, FID, security force assistance (SFA), military information support operations (MISO), and civil affairs operations (CAO).

In environments where the threat level posed by revisionist states is not high, ARSOF can establish relationships and knowledge that could be leveraged if support were needed in the future and can help host-nation forces develop resilience against threats such as illicit trafficking or ongoing territorial disputes. One primary benefit of these activities is that they can augment familiarization: By living and working in a foreign country, alongside foreign forces or other groups, ARSOF teams are able to further refine their understanding of an environment, whether physical or human. This type of information can be used, for example, to inform assessments for security cooperation planning, to shape combatant command or theater special operations command campaign plans, or, when specifically authorized, to respond to a combatant commander's priority intelligence requirements.[1] OIE, often conducted in conjunction with CAO, can provide utility in competitive environments, such as when civil affairs specialists perform face-to-face messaging with a vulnerable population during humanitarian or relief operations or other civil-military engagement.[2]

Further, security cooperation programs and exercises can also serve to assure U.S. allies and partners of the United States' commitment, while also deterring adversaries.[3] In what are often public shows

---

[1] Priority intelligence requirements are those requirements "that the commander and staff need to understand the adversary or other aspects of the operational environment" (Joint Chiefs of Staff, 2016, pp. 189–190).

[2] Following the practice of the Army's MDO concept, we generally refer to these operations as OIE. Joint Publication 3-05, *Special Operations*, does not use the term OIE in describing SOF's core activities and refers instead to information operations. Accordingly, we use the term *information operations* or its abbreviation, *IO*, when we are referring directly to the SOF core activity. We also use the term when referring to specific forces, as their formal career fields are still IO.

[3] See, for instance, Haddick, 2017.

of goodwill and capability development, the United States and participating foreign nations can demonstrate to other nations the strength of a partnership or alliance and the resolve of the United States (or other nations) to counter adversarial action in the region.

Certain partnering engagements are not intended to serve as public demonstrations of resolve and partner assurance, however. Even without impending armed conflict, U.S. involvement even in partnering or exercise activities can be politically sensitive and require lower visibility and smaller personnel footprints, requirements for which ARSOF can be well suited.

As the competitive space intensifies, some ARSOF activities are largely conducted to prepare for potential, or even anticipated, conflict (conventional or irregular), to disrupt them before they occur, and/or to generate resistance and resilience against malign actors when conflict occurs. UW, FID, and SFA almost always involve working alongside foreign partners, groups, or individuals, depending on the mission, but CAO and OIE do not necessarily require partner involvement: if authorities are available, U.S. forces can conduct these types of operations independently.[4] However, in the competitive space, U.S. CAO and MISO teams frequently work with partner forces, such as when U.S. teams advise foreign civil affairs forces to understand local dynamics in contested environments, or when MISO teams assist local or indigenous forces with operational or strategic messaging, such as U.S. MISO specialists' support to South Korean forces along the demilitarized zone amid tensions between Pyongyang and Seoul.[5]

Activities ARSOF might undertake in competitive environments can also have a deterrent effect on enemy actors, who might determine that increased hostile activity would not be worth the risk, and/or can signal assurance of U.S. support to key partners—which might be established foreign national forces, or irregular forces or groups who

---

4 Even in independently conducted CAO or OIE in competitive environments, U.S. forces generally would need to have permission from the host nation to conduct the activities.

5 Injoo Park, "Using PSYOP Against North Korea," Council on Foreign Relations, October 28, 2015.

constitute a viable guerrilla force.[6] However, these activities can be conducted in overt or covert manners, depending on mission requirements. Many clandestine activities would likely not have substantial deterrent effect in these environments, as they could aim to be undetected by adversaries.

Requirements

In the competition space, "winning" is challenging to define. As former U.S. Special Operations Command (USSOCOM) and U.S. Central Command (CENTCOM) commander Joseph L. Votel described,

> A Gray Zone "win" is not a win in the classic warfare sense. Winning is perhaps better described as maintaining the U.S. Government's positional advantage, namely the ability to influence partners, populations, and threats toward achievement of our regional or strategic objectives. Specifically, this will mean retaining decision space, maximizing desirable strategic options, or simply denying an adversary a decisive positional advantage.[7]

Although traditional victory cannot be attained, we can identify that successful competition largely requires that national institutions are equipped to withstand adversarial influences, that military forces have capabilities to deter and later disrupt malign activity, and that local populations are informed, engaged, and supportive of national goals.[8] One caveat is that in areas where UW is being conducted or is anticipated to be conducted, the ruling government or military force is likely to be the adversary. In that case, viable partners will in most cases be irregular forces, groups, or individuals conducting UW, so developing institutional resilience is different from overseeing formal national

---

6 For more information on SOF's role in deterring adversaries, see Haddick, 2017.

7 Votel et al., 2016, p. 108.

8 Brian W. James, "Sharpening the Spear of NATO SOF: Deterring Russian Hybrid Aggression Through Network Targeting," *Countering Terrorism Exchange*, Vol. 6, No. 4, 2016, p. 79.

forces and requires different approaches to enabling partners. Taken together, to prevail in the competitive space, the following conditions must be satisfied:[9]

- **Adversarial messaging and information efforts are mitigated, and counter-messaging efforts are effective.** Malign actors will attempt to shape public opinion to their favor and to discredit the host-nation government and its forces. Some of these efforts might be more robust and multifaceted in nature and focus on targeting key populations to generate support for adversary goals and efforts and to sow distrust of host-nation institutions. These types of efforts must be countered and minimized in the general public and in specific subpopulations that are more likely to be influenced by adversarial messaging efforts, and offensive OIE should be conducted to proactively shape the information environment.
- **Key populations are resistant to malign activity, and support friendly efforts.** To shape conditions without conducting high-end, overt operations, adversaries will seek to influence individual or group actors that are subject to coercion, corruption, or manipulation or are ideologically or culturally aligned with the adversarial state. These subpopulations must be resilient against efforts that aim to exploit disenchantment with the national government and generate support for adversary goals. In irregular warfare environments, adversaries will likely conduct multiple targeted efforts to coerce, corrupt, and/or manipulate local populations without overt violence, and/or appeal to those ideologically aligned with the adversary actor. To resist these efforts, challenges in these key populations must be addressed by credible host-nation institutions, and, beyond just demonstrating resilience to adversarial efforts, populations should be positively engaged in supporting friendly efforts.

---

9 For more information on what conditions need to be met to succeed in competition, see, for example, James, 2016, and Votel et al., 2016.

- **Decisionmakers are resilient against internal or external threats, including efforts to be influenced by malign actors.** In competitive environments, malign actors will attempt to shape (or, in some cases, constrain or derail) institutional decisionmaking processes and the officials who participate in those processes. These efforts could be made by external adversaries or internal actors who have been corrupted and/or influenced by malign actors. To guard against these threats, partner-nation civilian and military leadership must proactively guard against corruption, institutionalize practices and processes, and draw on support from the United States and other allies and partners, "in order to maintain the depth to govern, for protection against state adversaries operating in the Gray Zone, and nonstate actors seeking to destabilize states."[10]
- **Foreign partners are assured of U.S. resolve, while adversaries are deterred.** Adversarial actors will seek to lower a nation's confidence that it can rely on the United States and its partners in the event of a hostile incursion, and to present themselves as strong actors in the region. To counter these actions, and to preclude adversarial actors from positioning themselves as reliable partners, the United States and other nations must engage in measures that demonstrate commitment and resolve.
- **Partners of choice are enabled and willing to take action.** For overt requirements, exercises and training are conducted to show resolve and willingness to use force. Partners—regular or irregular, depending on the needs of the mission—are trained and equipped to execute missions. In addition, forces must have the will to conduct operations, at the tactical, operational, and strategic levels.
- **Adversarial networks are illuminated, tracked, and disrupted.** Because malign activity will constitute the cultivation of various actors and networks, potentially proxy networks, these actors must

---

[10] Becca Wasser, Ben Connable, Anthony Atler, and James Sladden, eds., *Comprehensive Deterrence Forum: Proceedings and Commissioned Papers*, Santa Monica, Calif.: RAND Corporation, CF-345-A, 2018, p. 5.

be identified and tracked. In many cases, local forces—military and/or civilian—will need to have capabilities to detect and track those networks, many of which might be clandestine or covert. These networks can include disenchanted government and military officials, resistance movements, and individual members of subpopulations that might be more subject to corruption and/or coercion. To combat these efforts, enabled military and/or civilian forces (whether state or nonstate actors) will need to be able to build on their detection and tracking capabilities, and be capable of disrupting those enemy networks (which can be foreign, domestic, or both).

Options

Several options are available to U.S. decisionmakers to pursue an advantage in the competitive environment. These activities are not necessarily mutually exclusive, but the conditions that favor one option might not benefit from the employment of another (e.g., the need for an overt show of U.S. resolve would likely not be most effectively satisfied by the deployment of a covertly operating ARSOF team).

Some of these activities can be conducted only by ARSOF (or other SOF personnel), whereas others are more appropriately conducted by conventional forces or other U.S. government actors. Many activities would benefit from coordinated efforts between ARSOF and non-ARSOF elements. In most cases, robust coordination and integration among ARSOF, conventional forces, and civilian agencies in executing these activities should occur to facilitate unity of effort and greatest impact.

Table 2.1 describes activities that can be conducted to succeed in competition, and characterizes the potential ARSOF and non-ARSOF roles in those activities. We derived these options from a broad range of doctrinal materials, unclassified planning documents, historical examples, and background interviews with practitioners. They are intended to be illustrative, not comprehensive. Decisionmakers typically attempt to limit risk in competitive environments. These options therefore primarily emphasize ways in which ARSOF can empower allies and partners to take action and ways in which ARSOF can lay the groundwork for more intensive activities should they be necessary.

Following the table, we analyze the advantages and disadvantages of employing conventional forces, other U.S. government agencies, and ARSOF as the lead actor in these capacities.

Advantages and Disadvantages of Potential Activities Led by ARSOF

Overall, ARSOF provide several advantages in executing activities in the competition space, as they are well suited to the smaller-scale, specialized, and lower-visibility activities that are often desired in this environment. Additionally, ARSOF have substantial experience with these types of activities. ARSOF's capabilities can also be leveraged as a complement to other ongoing conventional force and/or U.S. government activities in the intelligence, law enforcement, diplomacy, and information realms. However, the nature of ARSOF's size and small-footprint approach, while advantageous in many situations, can also pose challenges.

Advantages

First, ARSOF are trained to deliver outsized effects on forces much larger in size. Army Special Forces training, for example, enables forces to be adept in MDO concepts such as "denying or restricting the support provided by the adversary's conventional forces to proxies [to allow] U.S. partners to more easily counter attempts to destabilize their countries."[11] This allows ARSOF to deploy in small numbers to counter larger adversary forces, proxy or otherwise, while reducing cost and limiting visibility. ARSOF can also operate independently or in support of a larger conventional effort, though traditional conventional activities would likely be limited in the competition space, particularly in a UW campaign. Similarly, ARSOF can support U.S. government

---

[11] TRADOC, *The U.S. Army in Multi-Domain Operations 2028*, Fort Monroe, Va., 2018., p. viii.

Table 2.1
Illustrative List of Potential Competitive Activities

Requirement	Activities	ARSOF Role	Non-ARSOF Role
Adversarial messaging and information efforts are mitigated, and counter-messaging efforts are effective	• Build partner OIE unit capacity and operate alongside trained units • Conduct public diplomacy campaigns and multifaceted, targeted OIE campaigns with partner-nation forces to generate support for host-nation and/or U.S. goals • Develop and conduct OIE campaigns with partner-nation forces to generate support for host-nation and/or U.S. goals and counter a broad range of aggressive adversary information warfare efforts	• Develop partner forces' ability to design and conduct OIE operations, and conduct limited advise-and-assist activities in support of partner-nation OIE • Support and integrate with other agencies' public diplomacy and other counter-messaging efforts; support conventional cyberspace OIE activities • Work with partner-nation OIE units to develop and implement OIE campaigns across a range of OIE dimensions, focused on populations whose support is critical • Execute counter-messaging and other OIE campaigns with partner-nation OIE units	**Conventional military:** • Provide training and support to partner-nation forces in developing OIE capabilities • Conduct operations across multiple OIE disciplines in support of partner-nation efforts • Develop cyberspace OIE capabilities in partner-nation forces and develop and conduct cyberspace-oriented OIE campaigns; deter or preempt adversarial messaging through targeted and limited offensive cyber operations.[a] **Other:** • Provide messaging and other OIE support through means such as the Broadcasting Board of Governors and the Department of State's public diplomacy efforts and Global Engagement Center • Coordinate with nongovernmental organizations and host-nation media outlets • Implement sanctions against known adversarial IO actors to deter further operations

Table 2.1—continued

Requirement	Activities	ARSOF Role	Non-ARSOF Role
Key populations are resistant to malign activity and support friendly efforts	• Conduct outreach to civilian populations to generate positive civilian-military relations and elicit active support from local populations in efforts to counter malign influence • Develop partner civil affairs forces' capabilities and capacity and conduct partnered CAO • Provide civil assistance to specific populations to reduce vulnerability and increase resilience against known adversarial efforts	• Develop partner civil affairs forces' ability to identify and develop interventions to strengthen civilian-military relations • Conduct training with partner forces on effective civilian-military relations • Provide targeted civil affairs security assistance to counter specific threats to local populations posed by malign actors • Assist partner civil affairs forces in implementing interventions to strengthen civilian-military relations and generate active support from civilian populations • Provide short-term humanitarian assistance and other civil interventions to key populations	**Conventional military**: • Provide training to conventional foreign partners' civil affairs units to identify and develop interventions to strengthen civilian-military relations and on effective civilian-military relations • Provide humanitarian assistance to needed populations • In support of a larger campaign, assist conventional civil affairs forces to implement CAO interventions **Other:** • Provide civilian perspective in training on civilian-military relations • Provide short- and longer-term humanitarian and civil assistance to key populations
Decision-makers are resilient against internal or external threats, including efforts to be influenced by malign actors	• Conduct defense institution–building activities and anti-corruption activities, and pursue institutionalization of efforts • Conduct civilian institution–building activities and anti-corruption activities, and pursue institutionalization of efforts	• Establish, routinize, and expand exchange of high-profile subject-matter experts • Embed ARSOF advisors in foreign ministries • Establish a Special Operations Liaison Officer (SOLO) position to engage with foreign counterparts	**Conventional military:** • Engage in large-scale defense institution–building efforts (including anticorruption and institutionalization of efforts) • Establish exchanges of high-profile subject-matter expert • Embed advisors in foreign ministries **Other:** • Conduct civilian institution–building efforts (including anticorruption and institutionalization of efforts)

Table 2.1—continued

Requirement	Activities	ARSOF Role	Non-ARSOF Role
Foreign partners are assured of U.S. resolve, while adversaries are deterred	• Conduct security cooperation engagements or exercises to demonstrate U.S. commitment • Publicly message and provide overt evidence of U.S. resolve and support	• Conduct ARSOF-to-partner-SOF training, exercises and other security cooperation activities • Develop strategic messaging campaigns to publicly signal U.S. support and resolve • Participate in robust, conventional-led exercises	**Conventional military:** • Conduct more highly visible training, exercises and other security cooperation activities with conventional forces • Develop strategic messaging campaigns about U.S. support and resolve if a larger conventional effort is underway **Other:** • Support arms and other defense articles sales • Integrate security cooperation efforts with foreign assistance
Partners of choice are enabled and willing to take action	• Provide security assistance tailored to threats facing partner nation • Conduct partnered and supported operations against irregular threats	• Conduct ARSOF-to-partner-SOF capacity-building activities focused on countering irregular threats through a range of SOF activities • Conduct SOF-specific partnered and supported operations, such as intelligence campaigns against key adversaries and their networks • Lead low-visibility exercises and partner in UW efforts	**Conventional military:** • Conduct security cooperation and capability development with counterpart forces on conventional activities **Other:** • Support defense institution–building efforts • Provide intelligence analysis and support to partners

Table 2.1—continued

Requirement	Activities	ARSOF Role	Non-ARSOF Role
Adversarial networks are illuminated, tracked, and disrupted	• Conduct building partner capacity (BPC) activities with partner forces to augment organic network analysis capabilities • Assist partner forces to illuminate and disrupt adversary networks through irregular means • Detect and track adversary networks using U.S. assets	• Conduct security cooperation training activities and exercises with partner SOF on network illumination and disruption • Conduct irregular warfare operations with partner SOF to counter adversary networks through reconnaissance, tracking, and other activities • Conduct subject-matter-expert exchanges to share best practices in network analysis • Conduct low-visibility activities to illuminate and disrupt adversary networks and their activities • Identify and track networks by leveraging existing or new ARSOF-led analytic platforms, independently or through partners	**Conventional military:** • Conduct security cooperation activities and exercises to increase conventional counterpart forces' ability to develop and sustain a larger scale network disruption capability, including logistics and sustainment and other support elements **Other:** • Identify and track adversary networks using intelligence assets • Conduct low-visibility activities to gain clarity on adversary networks • Share intelligence

[a] For instance, U.S. Cyber Command in late 2018 disabled several computers that belonged to Russia's "troll farm" in an effort to deter that organization's anticipated operations to affect the U.S. 2018 midterm elections: Julian E. Barnes, "Cyber Command Operation Took Down Russian Troll Farm for Midterm Elections," *New York Times*, February 26, 2019.

activities in the intelligence, law enforcement, diplomacy, and information realms in competitive environments.

As is true in any environment, SOF are generally able to be employed more flexibly and quickly than conventional forces can be, which might be particularly useful under the time pressure demands that can characterize competition. Further, working by, with, and through partners is fundamental to SOF training and operations, and particularly ARSOF. ARSOF are specifically trained to learn local languages, understand cultural factors, and develop trust with foreign forces, groups, and individuals, among other competencies—all of which serve to support partnering efforts across the competitive environment. In some cases, partner nations might desire their forces to be trained and advised in the capabilities that ARSOF can provide but, for political reasons, do not want the assistance to be public. ARSOF presents as an ideal candidate for administering security cooperation engagements in such circumstances.

As environments edge from "ordinary" competition closer to armed conflict, the primary advantages that ARSOF offers over conventional forces and most U.S. government agencies are, first, its expertise in and authorities to conduct UW and, second, its ability to operate in denied environments.

First, UW can be a central activity in competition. UW is one of SOF's core activities, and a mainstay of specifically ARSOF's capabilities. ARSOF's experience in working by, with, and through foreign partners and in training on language and other cultural understanding provides a significant advantage when conducting UW activities, as the preparation for and execution of these operations is often reliant on coordination with and gaining the trust of foreign partners. Second, ARSOF are highly experienced in understanding and tracking a wide range of malign networks, from terrorist groups to proxy or uniformed national forces, to better understand their activities, intentions, and behaviors.[12]

Further, competition often requires clandestine operations, which ARSOF are well equipped to conduct in terms of capabilities and authorities. ARSOF also sometimes execute overt activities as well, though at a smaller scale than conventional forces can. By comparison, conventional forces and some other U.S. government agencies generally conduct only overt activities in the competitive space, and other U.S. government agencies conduct only clandestine or covert activities. Only ARSOF is commonly tasked to conduct both overt and clandestine operations, offering a significant advantage in terms of their agility and utility.

---

[12] James, 2016.

Because of these and other specific capabilities, ARSOF are sometimes granted different authorities and permissions than conventional forces are, and owing to these authorities, often can work more quickly and in a greater range of roles than conventional forces. Relative to other U.S. government organizations, ARSOF might also have substantially more resources to support competition activities.

Disadvantages

The nature of ARSOF's size and small-footprint approach, although advantageous in many situations, can also pose challenges. When deployed, ARSOF teams are generally quite small, especially compared with their conventional counterparts. The relatively small team size might be less useful if the main thrust of the effort is overt and/or intended to have deterrent effect.

Further, ARSOF's relatively small footprint in a given competitive environment can mean that their force protection assets are necessarily limited, given the need to keep numbers of personnel low in such contexts. If the presence of ARSOF personnel is exposed, this can pose challenges in protecting or facilitating their movement to a more secure location, if that is required. This can limit the extent of the personnel-intensive activities that ARSOF are able to execute, such as robust exercises, for the simple reason that there are fewer deployed personnel to participate in exercises. However, there are examples of larger ARSOF exercises that occur on an annual basis, depending on the area of responsibility.

Additionally, ARSOF are not designed to be entirely self-supporting over a long period of time. SOF generally rely heavily on conventional support for many SOF-led operations, such as for logistics, construction, engineering, and other typical support functions. This mitigates ARSOF's utility as a small-footprint option for long-term missions that require ongoing support from conventional forces; units can only deploy forward in a self-sustaining capacity for so long. However, many activities needed in a competitive environment might not require such a large, long-term presence.

Another potential weakness relative to other U.S. actors is that ARSOF, as well as conventional forces, are limited by the underlying authority that enables their presence in a particular country or region. For example, unless an authority specifies otherwise, SOF located in a particular country for a capabilities exercise are not permitted to conduct intelligence and reconnaissance missions. Teams are limited to recording and storing "atmospherics" information that is gained ancillary to other activities; targeted intelligence collection must be specifically authorized. Other U.S. government agencies might have broader authorities that enable more intensive collection activities.

More generally, most ARSOF are trained in multiple capabilities so they can be used in a variety of situations with a relatively small footprint. This agility clearly offers advantages, but it also means that personnel from other U.S. government agencies or conventional personnel might have higher levels of expertise in certain skills that might be critical in partnering efforts, such as language training. Likewise, ARSOF have relatively limited expertise in some support functions and strategic-level policy and planning, compared with conventional forces or other U.S. government personnel, which can have implications, especially if foreign partners require guidance in those areas. If such concentrated expertise is necessary, particularly in SFA and/or FID at the ministerial levels, some ARSOF personnel might not be suitable to meet the requirement.

Specific to OIE, one distinct disadvantage of ARSOF is that, while exhibiting robust OIE capabilities overall, they suffer from relative lack of expertise in cyberspace operations. Major General Kurt Sonntag, the commander of the Army's Special Operations Training Center of Excellence, claimed that SOF's cyber education was overwhelmingly nascent and defensively focused, adding that recruiting and retention problems hindered the ability to rapidly expand the ranks of specialists.[13] However the ARSOF community has taken steps to address this issue, especially as it relates to training.[14]

Finally, one substantial disadvantage to note is ARSOF's limited capacity to operate in all environments at once, because their expertise

---

[13] Todd South, "Cyber Skills Needed: Special Ops Leaders Seek Soldiers Who Can Fight the Enemy Up Close and Online," *Army Times*, October 3, 2017.

[14] South, 2017.

is in high demand in IW activities. The negative side of ARSOF's agility and utility to be employed in a number of different capacities means that the force can be seen as an "easy button" and, as a result, ARSOF may be overtasked or inappropriately tasked.[15]

Advantages and Disadvantages of Potential Activities Led by Conventional Forces

The main advantages of conventional forces are the size, resourcing, and concentration of expertise that they bring to bear in any environment. First, because of their size and the nature of their activities, conventional forces are better able to provide overt shows of U.S. resolve than ARSOF or other U.S. government agencies. Additionally, large units of conventional forces can deploy with a wide variety of capabilities that small ARSOF teams typically do not possess, such as their own logistics and sustainment capabilities and other institutional functions. Because of this breadth of experience, conventional forces are also better equipped to advise on and develop these support functions in foreign forces, which are critical capabilities in training a conventional military force to counter malign activity. Conventional forces are able to advise at the strategic, operational, and tactical levels, either in larger units or when deployed as individuals.

Conventional forces also conduct a wide range of security cooperation activities. These activities include BPC training and equipping programs, FID, binational or multinational exercises, subject-matter-expert technical exchanges, provision of embedded advisors in foreign ministries, and more. While these activities can be conducted by smaller, regionally aligned units or even by one- or two-person deployments (such as with technical exchanges or embedded advisors), conventional units can also conduct security cooperation activities in larger deployments. Certain conventional units, such as the Army's

---

[15] Kimberly Jackson, "U.S. Special Operations Command," in S. Rebecca Zimmerman, Kimberly Jackson, Natasha Lander, Colin Roberts, Dan Madden, and Rebeca Orrie, *Movement and Maneuver: Culture and the Competition for Influence Among the U.S. Military Services*, Santa Monica, Calif: RAND Corporation, RR-2270-OSD, 2019, p. 138.

security force assistance brigades (SFABs), are specifically designed for this mission. In addition to foreign language training, SFAB personnel "receive training on foreign weapons, advanced medical training, driver training, and survival, evasion, resistance, and escape (SERE) training."[16] These forces work primarily with another country's conventional security forces. This force construct is larger than those in ARSOF and requires a larger footprint. This means that SFABs offer an advantage over ARSOF or other U.S. government agencies in environments where conventional forces are deployed and visibility is not a major consideration, which is not necessarily the case in competition unless high visibility is specifically desired to signal deterrence or assurance. In that case, conventional forces are likely more effective, since the force constructs and platforms involved are generally far more visible and resource-intensive than ARSOF activities. However, when low-visibility security cooperation activities are desired, especially to develop ARSOF-specific skills, conventional forces, including SFABs, present fewer advantages than ARSOF.

Significantly, conventional forces generally do not conduct UW. In competition, UW might be a decisive tool to counter adversary actions. The nature of UW requires specific authorities, training, and experience not widely resident throughout the conventional forces, and often a smaller footprint than traditional conventional deployments do not create. Moreover, conventional forces generally cannot operate in denied environments the way that ARSOF and some other government agencies can. This has substantial implications, because such "frontline" access could prove significant or even required in denied environments.

Conventional civil affairs units are generally aligned to support deployed brigade combat teams and have the capacity to support larger conventional deployments. Despite being organized into similar small-team structures as ARSOF-aligned civil affairs units, conventional civil affairs battalions feature more headquarters-type elements because of their conventional mission. This means conventional civil affairs units

---

[16] Congressional Research Service, *Army Security Force Assistance Brigades*, Washington, D.C., October 24, 2018.

offer an advantage in terms of size and support when deployed in support of a larger-footprint, and higher-visibility, mission. However, the competitive environment might not support such a deployment, and conventional civil affairs teams might be more effectively used in support of ARSOF units. Indeed, conventional civil affairs forces often deploy in support of ARSOF missions. In that capacity, their capabilities are quite similar to those of ARSOF-aligned units. While ARSOF-aligned units might have more ARSOF-specific training in some cases, conventional civil affairs units are largely composed of Army Reserve personnel who have civilian expertise in a range of career fields useful to civil affairs operations, such as economics, public utilities, and agricultural development. These skills could prove to be advantageous in a range of civil affairs efforts but are reliant on the personal skills within a unit, which could vary.

In terms of OIE, conventional forces offer certain advantages. For example, like their civil affairs counterparts, conventional forces tasked with OIE are generally able to support larger conventional deployments, which are conducive to engagements of longer duration and can foster strong relationships with host-nation counterparts. However, in competition, such as mobilizations, conventional forces' relatively large footprint might not be desirable. Relatedly, conventional capabilities for OIE offer the advantages of greater number of personnel and associated resources. DoD requested $9.6 billion for cyber operations for fiscal year 2020, a billion-dollar increase from the 2019 request.[17] The department's expected budget for MISO in 2018 amounted to over $164 million, even after a significant decrease in operational contingency funding tied to Afghanistan.[18] Additionally, conventional forces retain greater cyber capabilities than ARSOF and can translate that expertise to combined OIE in partner nations or in training partner-nation information operations (IO) units on both traditional OIE

[17] Lauren C. Williams, "2020 Budget Boosts Funding for Cyber Forces, AI," *Defense Systems*, March 11, 2019.

[18] Approximately $25 million of that sum was allocated to SOCOM (Office of the Under Secretary of Defense [Comptroller], Chief Financial Officer, *Operation and Maintenance Overview, Fiscal Year 2018 Budget Estimates*, Washington, D.C.: U.S. Department of Defense, June 2017).

campaigns and cyber-centric campaigns. Of note, conventional Army PSYOP forces are exclusively reservists, whereas the Army's active duty PSYOP forces are dedicated to ARSOF support. This can mean, on the one hand, that conventional PSYOP forces are able to bring their civilian expertise to bear; on the other, reserve forces might be less available and/or less experienced in PSYOP deployments, for example, than their active duty counterparts supporting ARSOF.

Advantages and Disadvantages of Potential Activities Led by Other U.S. Government Agencies

Other U.S. government agencies, such as the Department of State, Department of Homeland Security (DHS), Federal Bureau of Investigation (FBI), and members of the Intelligence Community, can also provide decisionmakers with options to compete effectively. These agencies' personnel are highly skilled in critical areas that ARSOF and conventional forces are not, such as counter threat finance, economic development, civilian institution–building, project management, and intelligence analysis, and those skills might be highly useful in FID or SFA activities, for example.

Also, in addition to active conflict areas, other U.S. government agencies have authorities to allow their presence in nations where the threat of active conflict is low. This presence allows for access to and information about areas that would not otherwise be available to military forces and enables the development of key relationships with foreign leaders that might not be developed through military channels. However, depending on the circumstances, some areas in competitive environments might be denied and difficult for many U.S. government agencies to access.

Further, other U.S. government agencies also conduct types of security cooperation activities that are likely not suitable for military forces to execute. The Department of State, for example, conducts security assistance and other nation-building activities, and other relevant U.S. government agencies, such as the FBI and DHS, conduct partnering activities with their foreign equivalents. This can allow crucial partnerships and capabilities to be developed in nonmilitary elements of a foreign nation, such as intelligence agencies or ministries of foreign affairs, that are critical to security goals. As another example, the U.S. Agency for International Development (USAID) has substantial experience in activities that closely resemble or align with CAO, but USAID's projects are typically of much longer duration. For OIE, other government agencies, such as the State Department, have experience in conducting relevant activities in competitive environments.[19] Further, some agencies also support significant budgets to develop their programs, including those in Europe. The State Department's public diplomacy budget for Europe and Eurasia in fiscal year (FY) 2017, for instance, totaled more than $190 million, and the State Department's Global Engagement Center received approximately $75 million in funding for FY 2019.[20] However, in many of these agencies, OIE-relevant departments typically support other priorities, and larger budgets do not necessarily translate into more efficient or effective operations. The Global Engagement Center, for instance, suffered from confusing organizational changes and an unclear mandate from its inception through at least 2018, despite additional funding.[21] Further, since the disbandment of the U.S. Information Agency in 1999, some say the State Department has been challenged to integrate public diplomacy into its broader work.[22]

---

19 For example, Radio Free Europe/Radio Liberty, a multilingual news outlet covering events in Europe and Eurasia, is currently run through the U.S. Broadcasting Board of Governors and boasted an audience of 33.9 million per week to its broadcasts and publications in fiscal year 2018 (Radio Free Europe/Radio Liberty, "About Us," undated).

20 U.S. Advisory Commission on Public Diplomacy, *2018 Comprehensive Annual Report on Public Diplomacy and International Broadcasting*, Washington, D.C.: U.S. Department of State, 2019; U.S. Senate, Committee on Appropriations, *Department of State, Foreign Operations, and Related Programs Appropriations Bill, 2019, Report 115-282*, Washington, D.C.: U.S. Government Printing Office, 2018.

21 Guy Taylor, "State Department Global Engagement Center Targets Russian Propaganda, 'Deep Fakes,'" Associated Press, December 12, 2018.

22 Matthew Armstrong, "No, We Do Not Need to Revive the U.S. Information Agency," *War on the Rocks*, November 12, 2015.

Certain U.S. government agencies are able to provide UW support to partners under more expansive authorities that have the potential to enable greater access and impact than ARSOF activities can. In the agencies that can provide UW support, personnel have high levels of training and expertise that can rival or exceed that in ARSOF. However, this capability is not resident in all U.S. government agencies, so UW capacity is still relatively limited across non-SOF actors.

In terms of civil affairs and similar activities, USAID, and specifically its Office of Transition Initiatives and the Office of Foreign Disaster Assistance, is practiced in operating in competitive environments to execute development projects that might be similar in nature to, or attempt to reach the same populations as, conventional or ARSOF CAO. USAID's experience in these activities is substantial, and civil affairs teams are often closely integrated with USAID teams abroad. However, as with other civilian agencies, USAID is generally less well resourced than military forces, and, because of their civilian nature, USAID personnel might not partner as naturally with other nations' military civil affairs teams as U.S. military teams can. Nongovernment civilian organizations can also operate in competitive environments, but they might be reluctant to partner with military units, seeking to preserve their civilian image.

Other U.S. government agencies have different purposes than the military does, which means they have different legal authorities to conduct certain activities. In some cases, these authorities can allow for options that the military cannot execute, in terms of type of activity (law enforcement partnerships, for example), how activities are executed (such as being directly embedded with a partner force versus serving only in a headquarters advisory capacity), and location of activity (such as outside a national capital, if military forces are required to remain within city limits). In other cases, however, military forces might have more appropriate authorities to operate in a competitive environment, depending on the location and the conditions. This mismatch of authorities underscores the importance of interagency coordination and collaboration to best understand who is poised to lead on specific activities, and how agencies can support one another.

One notable disadvantage of activities led by other U.S. government agencies is that these organizations generally have far less capacity and resourcing than military forces do, whether conventional or ARSOF. Military forces have larger budgets, more personnel, and, because of substantial support and infrastructure based on this capacity, often have greater ability to project into remote and contested areas. Relatedly, many other U.S. government agencies have limited expeditionary capability, due to multiple factors, such as their smaller budgets, limited force protection assets, and differing organizational missions. These limitations can create challenges in the nonpermissive or semipermissive areas that can characterize competitive environments.

CHAPTER THREE

The Potential Effectiveness of ARSOF Operations in Strategic Competition

It is impossible to fully evaluate each of the activities and options discussed in the previous chapter. Rather than focusing on each requirement for successful competition and the options the United States could employ in pursuit of these requirements, in this chapter we focus on several broad categories of activities or operations that ARSOF are frequently called on to perform: security cooperation, FID, UW,[1] and OIE.

For each type of activity, we either reviewed previous statistical analyses of their effectiveness or we extended prior statistical work. Because of the difficulties of acquiring full and accurate data on ARSOF deployments, most of the analyses reviewed here do not focus specifically on ARSOF. Given the characteristics of ARSOF and the types of activities that are found to be effective, however, it is possible to make informed estimates of the effectiveness of ARSOF, at least in general terms. In addition to these statistical analyses, we provide short vignettes on ARSOF activities to illustrate their uses and limitations.

Overall, the evidence from these reviews of and extensions of prior statistical analyses, combined with the vignettes here, suggests that ARSOF can play a valuable role in competition, but the empirical record is a nuanced one.

---

[1] ARSOF may also be called on to perform missions such as special reconnaissance or direct action. It is nearly impossible to discuss such activities in an publicly available publication, however, so we do not address them directly, although they may play a role in supporting the activities that we do analyze.

Security Cooperation

The United States undertakes security cooperation activities in pursuit of a number of goals, including building the military capacity of its allies and partners, assuring these allies and partners while deterring others, and preparing its own forces to operate in a wide range of environments. To assess effectiveness, we review findings on security cooperation's effectiveness in building capacity and in assurance and deterrence. Again, because publicly available data on ARSOF activities are highly limited, we review studies of security cooperation more broadly, although we also discuss reasons why we believe these findings are relevant to ARSOF.

Building Capacity

Security cooperation can help to build partners' capabilities across warfighting functions such as movement and maneuver, fires, mission command, intelligence, sustainment, and protection. It can also help to develop their capacity for security governance at the ministerial and general staff level and potentially influence their preferences concerning civil-military relations, respect for human rights, and other elements of fielding a professional military force.

There is considerable anecdotal evidence that security cooperation can help to build partners' military capabilities, especially at the tactical level and in the short term. The Iraqi Counter Terrorism Service (CTS), for instance, was built in close cooperation with ARSOF, and CTS is widely agreed to have provided the most effective forces for reversing Islamic State of Iraq and the Levant (ISIL) military gains (see Box 3.1).

Smaller-footprint advisory missions in countries such as Colombia, Kenya, and the Philippines have similarly been hailed as at least partial success stories.[2] It is difficult to acquire systematic and rigorous evidence on the fighting effectiveness of foreign militaries (absent a

---

[2] See, for instance, Linda Robinson, Patrick B. Johnston, and Gillian S. Oak, *U.S. Special Operations Forces in the Philippines, 2001–2014*, Santa Monica, Calif.: RAND Corporation, RR-1236-OSD, 2016.

Box 3.1. The Iraqi Counter Terrorism Service

The United States, primarily through the involvement of SOF, helped to build Iraq's Counter Terrorism Service (CTS) during the U.S. occupation of the country following the 2003 invasion. As its name suggests, the CTS was originally developed to target high-value terrorist and insurgent leaders. Over time, however, the CTS grew into the most capable security service in Iraq and played a critical role in defending the country from the Islamic State. Although the operational success of the CTS and its crucial role in liberating Iraqi cities from ISIS control is well documented, less well understood is the CTS's benefit to the United States as Washington competes with Tehran for influence in Iraq. Indeed, as the Islamic State threatened Baghdad, Iran leveraged Iraq's vulnerability to extend its influence. The CTS became one of the United States' primary contributions to Iraq's security and thus its ability to at least partially resist Iranian pressure.

SOF's Role and Activities

Among SOF, U.S. Army Special Forces had the lead in training and mentoring of CTS personnel, as well as partnering with CTS for missions when the United States was engaged with Iraqi Security Forces in an advise, assist, and accompany capacity.[a] It is difficult to overstate U.S. Army Special Forces' involvement in the creation and development of the CTS.[b]

One of the most important features of SOF's role was the continuous American engagement with SOF, featuring repeat deployments of the same American trainers, which resulted in strong relationships that allowed the CTS to remain mostly resilient to politicization while other Iraqi forces succumbed to that pull. U.S. Army Special Forces also used American training requirements (e.g., marksmanship tests) when training their Iraqi counterparts and strictly enforced qualification thresholds.[c] The United States also consciously pushed for the recruitment and retention of a multi-sectarian and multi-ethnic force. The inclusion of Kurdish and Sunni Arab members of the CTS, including in senior leadership positions, was viewed as a particularly important hedge against the CTS evolving into a sectarian instrument.

Outcomes and Implications

Modeled on U.S. Army Special Forces doctrine, the CTS became a professional force capable of conducting small-unit counterterrorism activity, and, as circumstances changed, the CTS repurposed its capabilities to meet the threat. After the rise of ISIL, that meant using its capabilities as an assault force on an entrenched enemy.

U.S. input into the design of the CTS as a professional, nonsectarian unit has also made it a natural partner in blunting the influence of Iran. The CTS provides a reliable force that decreases Iraq's dependence on Iranian-directed Shi'a militia. The evolution of the CTS demonstrates

Box 3.1—continued

some of the positive unintended consequences of prior security force assistance to the current U.S. priority of competing with regional and extra-regional powers.

To be sure, the CTS has not always operated as an ideal model for partner security forces. When Prime Minister Nouri al-Maliki increasingly reverted to sectarian rule from 2008 to 2014 in a bid to consolidate power, the CTS showed some signs of backsliding and was implicated in the prime minister's crackdowns on political opposition. In addition, relying on the CTS as a means to blunt Iranian influence in Iraq also introduces the risk of perpetuating the country's internal conflict.[d] But, overall, the CTS can be judged a success based on its operational contributions and its role as a balancer to the popular mobilization units and other elements of the Iraqi Security Forces (in particular, the Ministry of Interior Forces) that show strong affinity to Iran.

---

[a] Other components of U.S. SOF have assisted with the training of the force, as well as accompanying CTS in its missions. See Austin Long, Todd C. Helmus, S. Rebecca Zimmerman, Christopher M. Schnaubelt, and Peter Chalk, *Building Special Operations Partnerships in Afghanistan and Beyond: Challenges and Best Practices from Afghanistan, Iraq, and Colombia*, Santa Monica, Calif.: RAND Corporation, RR-713-OSD, 2015.

[b] David Witty, *The Iraqi Counter Terrorism Service*, Washington, D.C.: Brookings Institution, 2014, p. 7.

[c] Witty, 2014.

[d] International Crisis Group, *Loose Ends: Iraq's Security Forces Between U.S. Drawdown and Withdrawal*, Brussels, Belgium: ICG Middle East Report No. 99, October 2010.

war in which their capabilities become more apparent). Despite these data limitations, some prior RAND research undertaken across 29 partner countries suggests a broader base of support for claims that security cooperation can build military capabilities, especially tactical ones.[3] What is more contested is the ability of security cooperation to yield enduring, strategic gains. For improvements in military capabilities to lead to durable improvements in a country's strategic objectives, improvements must be both sustained over time and effectively

---

[3] Christopher Paul, Colin P. Clarke, Beth Grill, Stephanie Young, Jennifer D. P. Moroney, Joe Hogler, and Christine Leah, *What Works Best When Building Partner Capacity and Under What Circumstances?* Santa Monica, Calif: RAND Corporation, MG-1253/1-OSD, 2013.

harnessed to an appropriate political-military strategy. Among better-governed allies and partners, such as the Baltic states, capability gains are more likely to endure (see Box 3.2).

Sustainability requires highly capable security governance. For instance, defense institutions must be able to pass along tactics, techniques, and procedures learned from American trainers and advisors to other units and to future recruits. Defense institutions must be able to formulate budgets strategically, acquire materiel and maintain facilities without major losses to corruption, manage inventories of critical materiel, and that ensure units have access to this materiel in a timely manner. Nor is security governance solely the responsibility of defense institutions: Legislatures must be able to allocate the necessary funds, legislatures and courts must exercise effective oversight, and so on. Clearly, these requirements are both challenging and extend well beyond the ability of ARSOF alone to support.

Translating improvements in military capabilities into strategic gains also requires effective political leadership. Political leaders who worry more about coups than external military threats are likely to undermine the effectiveness of their armed forces.[4] Leaders who use violence indiscriminately against perceived internal enemies are likely to create more foes than they eliminate.[5]

Obviously, different partner countries are likely to define their strategic objectives differently. A comprehensive test of the strategic impact of security cooperation is thus likely infeasible. Prior RAND research, however, has tested the ability of security cooperation to contribute to domestic stability and reduce levels of internal political violence—perhaps the most important outcome of interest when considering how the United States can help protect partners from irregular threats in the competition space. In the widest-ranging RAND

---

[4] See, for instance, James T. Quinlivan, "Coup-Proofing: Its Practice and Consequences in the Middle Est," *International Security*, Vol. 24, No. 2, Fall 1999.

[5] See, for instance, Matthew Adam Kocher, Thomas B. Pepinsky, and Stathis N. Kalyvas, "Aerial Bombing and Counterinsurgency in the Vietnam War," *American Journal of Political Science*, Vol. 55, No. 2, April 2011; and Monica Duffy Toft and Yuri M. Zhukov, "Denial and Punishment in the North Caucasus: Evaluating the Effectiveness of Coercive Counterinsurgency," *Journal of Peace Research*, Vol. 49, No. 6, 2012.

Box 3.2. Building Unconventional Warfare Capacity in the Baltics

The Baltic nations of Estonia, Latvia, and Lithuania are the NATO allies most highly exposed to possible Russian aggression. Unsurprisingly, they have consistently advocated for greater deterrent presence from NATO and especially the United States since the Russian invasion of Ukraine in 2014. Decisionmakers in Washington and other Western capitals, however, want to underscore the NATO alliance's resolve and improve its capabilities for resisting both conventional and irregular aggression without taking actions that would precipitate escalating tensions or, in the worst case, a war with Russia.

ARSOF by themselves offer relatively little capability for resisting a conventional Russian invasion. They are, however, ideal for helping the Baltic states develop their own capabilities for deterring Russian use of "little green men" and, in the worst case, conducting irregular resistance to a Russian occupation force. Moreover, the Baltic states are highly capable allies—precisely the sort of partners the evidence suggests should be capable of sustaining any capability gains that ARSOF help to develop.

ARSOF's Role and Activities

SOF deployed to the Baltics participate in three types of activities: exercises, training, and joint deployments. The main exercise organized by Special Operations Command Europe (SOCEUR) in the region is Trojan Footprint, which is held biennially with the participation of Allied and partner forces from Europe. The purpose of Trojan Footprint is to improve interoperability and train the skills that ARSOF can contribute to Allied defense and resistance. The United States also regularly participates in the Lithuanian annual SOF exercise Flaming Sword, which focuses on developing interagency cooperation. SOF elements also participate in exercises to train allied conventional military force units, including the Estonian national exercise Hedgehog in 2018, Saber Junction 18, and Operation Rapid Forge in 2019. These exercises allow for mutual trust-building, exchange of information, and training of allied forces. Since 2013, SOCEUR has also sponsored international resistance seminars, which provide a forum to discuss UW, resistance movements, and partisan warfare and to create a common understanding. Another means of engagement has been Baltic states SOF deployments with their U.S. counterparts.[a]

Outcomes and Implications

The ARSOF presence in the Baltics serves several purposes: signaling the support of the United States to the deterrence and defense of the Baltic states; training the local forces; developing interoperability between the U.S. forces, the three host nations, and other allied forces; and building relationships and expanding ARSOF's knowledge of the region. Training

Box 3.2—continued

with their Baltic counterparts also helps ARSOF prepare for the type of UW warfare that could be expected in Europe.

Improving partners' UW and resistance capabilities has helped to develop these allies' capabilities for resisting foreign invasion and occupation, thus potentially helping deter Russian aggression. Despite low media coverage in the region, the presence of SOF and conventional exercises is considered to be a signal to the Kremlin that an incursion into a sovereign NATO country would trigger a resolute response from the United States and other NATO allies. U.S.-led exercises and participation in the region are viewed as a particularly powerful deterrent because of U.S. forces' capabilities and ability to react fast. However, while Baltic leaders have welcomed such assistance as part of a broader package of NATO support, it is more difficult to determine the extent to which these activities help to deter Moscow.[b]

---

[a] Michael Weisman, "NATO, Partner Spec Ops Forces Rapidly Deploy for Trojan Footprint 18," Air National Guard website, June 12, 2018; Tatyana White-Jenkins, "Exercise Hedgehog," *Citizen-Soldier*, October 5, 2018; "Saber Junction 2018 Integrated NATO, Partner SOF with Conventional Forces," *Army Recognition*, October 30, 2018; "Largest Baltic Special Forces Exercise Flaming Sword 2015 Culminates in Combined Operation," *Baltic Times*, June 4, 2015.

[b] Steven J. Flanagan, Jan Osburg, Anika Binnedijk, Marta Kepe, and Andrew Radin, *Deterring Russian Aggression in the Baltic States Through Resilience and Resistance*, Santa Monica, Calif.: RAND Corporation, RR-2779-OSD, 2019.

analysis of U.S. security cooperation,[6] researchers found that security cooperation contributed to small but statistically significant improvements in partners' internal stability, as measured by the State Fragility Index developed at the University of Maryland. However, this relationship was mediated by several important contextual factors. In general, countries that were more economically developed and better governed were able to make much more effective use of U.S. security sector assistance. Security cooperation was associated with gains in stability in Europe, the Asia-Pacific, and Latin America but not in the Middle

---

[6] Michael J. McNerney, Angela O'Mahony, Thomas S. Szayna, Derek Eaton, Caroline Baxter, Colin P. Clarke, Emma Cutrufello, Michael McGee, Heather Peterson, Leslie Adrienne Payne, and Calin Trenkov-Wermuth, *Assessing Security Cooperation as a Preventive Tool*, Santa Monica, Calif.: RAND Corporation, RR-350-A, 2014.

East or Africa, which have high concentrations of poor governance and low economic development.

These results are not specific to ARSOF security cooperation activities, but this finding does have implications for ARSOF. McNerney et al. found that the most effective types of security cooperation were those involving training and education—the focus of ARSOF activities—rather than materiel transfers. A related RAND report focusing more narrowly on Africa found no overall relationship in the post–Cold War era between security cooperation and several measures of political violence, including the onset of civil wars and insurgencies and terrorist attacks.[7] Of particular concern to a new era of great-power competition, Watts et al. found that U.S. military aid during the Cold War was actually associated with higher incidence of civil wars and insurgencies. But, more hopefully, they also found that security cooperation was associated with statistically significant declines in the incidence of wars, terrorist attacks, and state repression when it was provided in the context of a UN peace operation. The authors did not rigorously test the precise reasons for these relationships. But these findings are consistent with the security sector reform literature, which argues that lasting gains in stability derive in large part from long-term, persistent engagement—a hallmark of ARSOF cooperative activities.

Our discussion so far has focused on prior RAND research, as it is some of the most comprehensive and relevant to an understanding of what ARSOF can accomplish in strategic competition. There are several other studies, however, that also examine these issues rigorously. For the most part, they yield similar findings. Several non-RAND studies, for instance, have found that favorable outcomes (usually small but statistically significant nonetheless) tend to result from training

---

[7] Stephen Watts, Trevor Johnston, Matthew Lane, Sean Mann, Michael J. McNerney, and Andrew Brooks, *Building Security in Africa: An Evaluation of U.S. Security Sector Assistance in Africa from the Cold War to the Present*, Santa Monica, Calif.: RAND Corporation, RR-2447-OSD, 2018.

and education activities, while arms transfers are often associated with adverse effects on domestic political stability.[8]

Again, none of these findings are specific to ARSOF, but the characteristics associated with successful security cooperation are among those for which ARSOF are best known. ARSOF provide training and education—the types of security cooperation most closely associated with gains in domestic political stability. And ARSOF are able to work closely with partner forces over long periods of time, often returning to the same countries repeatedly and for lengthy deployments.[9] This persistent presence was also found to be one element of successful security cooperation, especially in more fragile states. Where ARSOF are often at a comparative disadvantage is in ministerial and higher-echelon sustainment functions, which are also critical to the success of security cooperation. Consequently, ARSOF can provide one key element for security cooperation impact, but they are most effective when deployed in conjunction with a broader initiative to build partner capacity and influence partner organizational culture, one that involves conventional forces and civilian partners from other parts of the U.S. government.

Assurance and Deterrence

Assessing the effects of ARSOF security cooperation activities on assurance of allies and partners and deterrence of potential adversar-

---

[8] See, for instance, Shannon Lindsey Blanton, "Foreign Policy in Transition? Human Rights, Democracy, and U.S. Arms Exports," *International Studies Quarterly*, Vol. 49, No. 4, December 2005; Sabrina M. Karim and William A. Wagstaff, "Keeping the Peace after Peacekeeping: How Peacekeepers Resolve the Security Dilemma in Post-Conflict States," unpublished paper, undated; and Tomislav Z. Ruby and Douglas Gibler, "US Professional Military Education and Democratization Abroad," *European Journal of International Relations*, Vol. 16, No. 3, 2010. For a contrary view, see Jesse Dillon Savage and Jonathan Caverley, "When Human Capital Threatens the Capitol: Foreign Aid in the Form of Military Training and Coups," *Journal of Peace Research*, Vol. 54, No. 4, 2017. For a broader review of the relevant literature, see Watts et al., 2018, and Stephen Watts, *Identifying and Mitigating Risks in Security Sector Assistance for Africa's Fragile States*, Santa Monica, Calif.: RAND Corporation, RR-808-A, 2015.

[9] For a discussion of the importance of the sort of persistent engagement ARSOF provides, see Simon J. Powelson, "Enduring Engagement Yes, Episodic Engagement No: Lessons for SOF from Mali," master's thesis, Monterey, Calif.: Naval Postgraduate School, December 2013.

ies is even more difficult than assessing capacity-building efforts. If a potential adversary does not attack, it is difficult for the analyst to determine whether that was because it was deterred or because it had no intention of attacking. Despite these challenges, the general logic of deterrence and past empirical work on deterrence can help to shed light on the role of ARSOF.

Deterrence theory suggests that for an external power to deter an attack on one of its allies or partners, two conditions must be met: First, the deterring power must demonstrate the capability to defend its ally or partner, and, second, the deterring power must demonstrate its commitment or willingness to support the ally or partner. In the deterrence literature, commitment or intent is typically communicated through so-called costly signals—that is, actions that are so costly for the would-be deterrer that only a highly committed power would undertake them.[10]

ARSOF can contribute to communicating both capability and intent, but they are not an ideal instrument to demonstrate either, at least by themselves. In any given year, ARSOF operate in many dozens of countries. Their mere presence, therefore, demonstrates little about the priority the United States places on a specific country in which they are operating, unless their presence is particularly large and extended. Moreover, because they often operate in a low-visibility manner, they do not make a strong statement about the United States' commitment; the United States could withdraw ARSOF personnel from low-visibility activities without the same loss of prestige that would accompany backing down from a larger, much more visible commitment. Finally, ARSOF are intended to be highly mobile. ARSOF can be quickly redeployed from one commitment to another, unlike, for instance, an armored brigade. Prior studies of deterrence have generally found that larger, heavier deployments that cannot be easily moved

---

[10] For an overview of this literature, see Paul K. Huth, "Deterrence and International Conflict: Empirical Findings and Theoretical Debates," *Annual Review of Political Science*, Vol. 2, 1999.

elsewhere seem to demonstrate the highest level of commitment and thus have the strongest effects on deterrence.[11]

ARSOF do, however, contribute to deterrence in ways that are different from larger, conventional deployments, and, in some cases, they may represent a superior alternative. First, because they are highly mobile, they can quickly deploy to a region at a time of crisis. Second, because they are trained to work by, with, and through partner forces, they can help to maximize the capabilities of a partner nation's forces, which may be better positioned and more motivated to protect their homeland than U.S. forces. Finally, ARSOF may represent a better deterrent against irregular threats than U.S. conventional forces because they have specialized capabilities for defeating precisely such threats.

Foreign Internal Defense

FID overlaps with security cooperation activities. In this section, we focus more specifically on FID when employed in active conflict zones in which a hostile power employs proxies or surrogates to conduct armed operations against a U.S. ally or partner.

As with our discussion of security cooperation, data limitations forced us to rely on an indirect approach for analyzing potential ARSOF effectiveness in FID. Building on prior RAND analysis, we analyzed military interventions on behalf of governments waging civil conflicts within their borders in the period since World War II. More specifically, we assessed whether the intervention of foreign military personnel on behalf of a government—independent of other factors—

---

11 See especially Bryan Frederick, Stephen Watts, Matthew Lane, Abby Doll, Ashley L. Rhoades, and Meagan L. Smith, *Understanding the Deterrent Impact of U.S. Overseas Forces*, Santa Monica, Calif.: RAND Corporation, RR-2533-A, 2018; Barry M. Blechman and Stephen S. Kaplan, *Force Without War: United States Armed Forces as a Political Instrument*, Washington, D.C.: Brookings Institution Press, 1978; and David E. Johnson, Karl P. Mueller, and William H. Taft, *Conventional Coercion Across the Spectrum of Operations: The Utility of U.S. Military Forces in the Emerging Security Environment*, Santa Monica, Calif.: RAND Corporation, MR-1494-A, 2003.

helps the government defeat insurgents supported by a hostile government. Although we did not evaluate the role of ARSOF alone, we did conduct separate analyses of U.S.-led operations, and we looked at the effects of the size of foreign deployments (the military "footprint") to distinguish the effects of the small-footprint operations characteristic of ARSOF.

In this analysis, we leveraged data on 250 episodes of civil war from 1946 to 2014. Drawing on multiple datasets, we identified 57 instances of military interventions on behalf of governments in those wars. We also determined instances of support for rebels in these wars. Utilizing this relatively rich dataset, we were able to compare not only the outcomes of intervention relative to non-intervention, but also the force levels associated with these outcomes. Additionally, we were able to weigh the likelihood of successful government interventions in the presence of countervailing interventions on behalf of the rebel side. This offers a more realistic assessment of great-power competition, at least in civil wars. The details of our statistical analyses can be found in a technical appendix at the end of this report.[12]

Figure 3.1 shows how great-power support (i.e., the United States, Russia, or China) to rebels affects the predicted probability of conflicts ending in a decisive outcome that is at least minimally acceptable to the government—that is, government victory or a negotiated

---

[12] Our analysis covers 250 episodes of violent conflict from 1946 through 2014, drawing from the Uppsala Conflict Data Program–Peace Research Institute Oslo (UCDP/PRIO) Armed Conflict Dataset (ACD) (UCDP/PRIO Armed Conflict Dataset, 2009; Nils Petter Gleditsch, Peter Wallensteen, Mikael Eriksson, Margareta Sollenberg, and Håvard Strand, "Armed Conflict 1946–2001: A New Dataset," *Journal of Peace Research*, Vol. 39, No. 5, 2002). In the ACD, conflict is defined as "a contest incompatibility that concerns government and/or territory . . . of which at least one [party] is the government of a state." We limited our analysis to conflicts reaching at least 1,000 battle-related deaths. Because the data are in country-year format, we converted this information into war episodes based on the start and end dates of each conflict. This process generated 250 civil war episodes for our statistical analyses. The outcomes of each conflict episode come from the political scientist Joakim Kreutz's conflict termination classification of the ACD (Joakim Kreutz, "How and When Armed Conflicts End: Introducing the UCDP Conflict Termination Dataset," *Journal of Peace Research*, Vol. 47, No. 2, 2010). These outcomes include government victory, rebel victory, negotiated settlement, and "low activity."

Figure 3.1
Predicted Probability of Conflict Outcomes, With and Without Support from Great Powers to Rebels

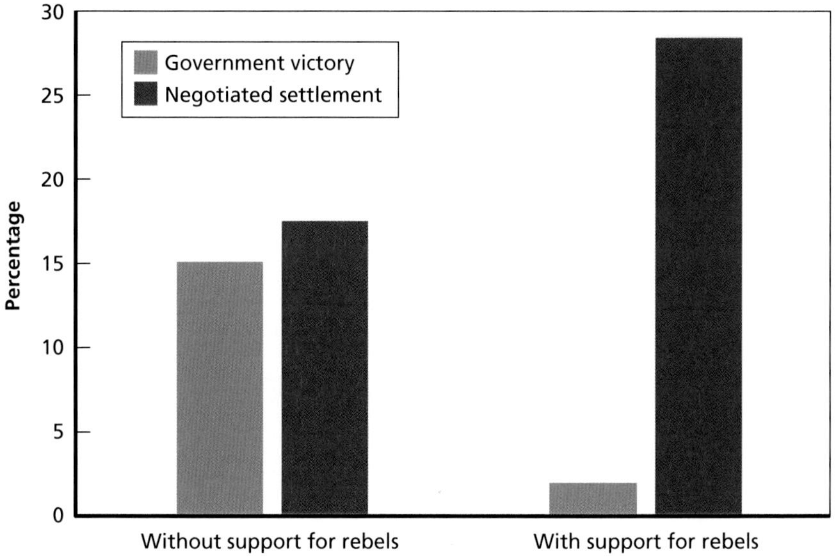

SOURCES: ACD; Non-State Actor dataset (NSA) (David E. Cunningham, Kristian Skrede Gleditsch, and Idean Salehyan, "Non-State Actors in Civil Wars: A New Dataset," *Conflict Management and Peace Science*, Vol. 30, No. 5, 2013a, pp. 516–531; and David E. Cunningham, Kristian Skrede Gleditsch, and Idean Salehyan, Non-State Actor dataset, version 3.4, 2013b); Kreutz, 2010; and authors' calculations.

settlement at least minimally satisfactory to all parties.[13] When great powers support rebels in civil conflicts, the chances of government victories fall precipitously. As indicated by the green bars, in the absence of rebel support by the United States, Russia (Soviet Union), or China, the predicted probability of government victory falls from just over 15 percent to approximately 2 percent. However, an opposite pattern emerges when looking at the odds of a negotiated settlement in the presence and absence of support to rebels. As shown by the purple

[13] Our primary analyses focused on only rebel support provided by the United States, Soviet Union or Russia, and China. As a robustness check, we assessed models including support to rebels from Iran and Cuba; including these additional countries did not meaningfully change the results.

bars, the predicted probability of a negotiated settlement rises from just under 18 percent (in absence of rebel support) to nearly 29 percent (when rebels receive support).

While great-power support for insurgents can significantly alter the likely outcomes of a civil war, military interventions on behalf of governments also affect these outcomes. Figure 3.2 shows the predicted probabilities of two conflict outcomes (government victory and negotiated settlement) by the size of the FID footprint, measured in troop numbers. The horizontal axis divides troops sizes into four categories: no substantial troop presence (i.e., fewer than 100 foreign troops in support of the government), 100 to 2,000 troops, 2,001 to 5,000 troops, and greater than 5,000 troops. Interestingly, the model

Figure 3.2
Predicted Probability of Conflict Outcomes by Size of Deployment for Foreign Internal Defense

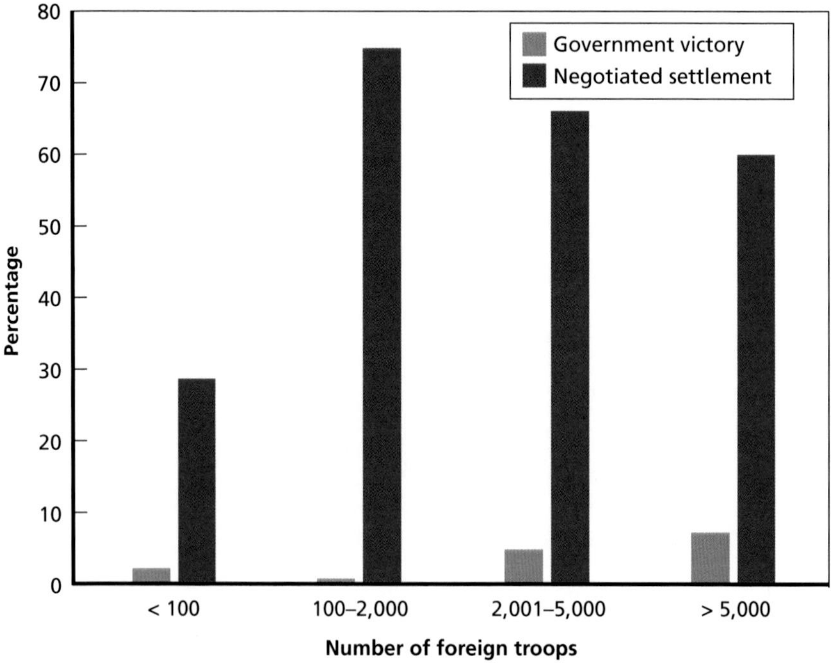

SOURCES: ADC; NSA; Kreutz, 2010; and authors' calculations.

results suggest that small numbers of forces in a FID role are associated with very modest increases in the odds of government victory but *dramatic* increases in the odds of negotiated settlements, even when rebels receive military support from great powers.

We are able to unpack this result a bit more by looking at the marginal impacts of increasing troop numbers on our outcomes of interest. Figure 3.3 displays the percentage-point change in the estimated probability of a government victory or a negotiated settlement for every

Figure 3.3
Percentage Point Change in Probability of Government Victory or Negotiated Settlement, per 1,000-Soldier Increase in Maximum Troops Level

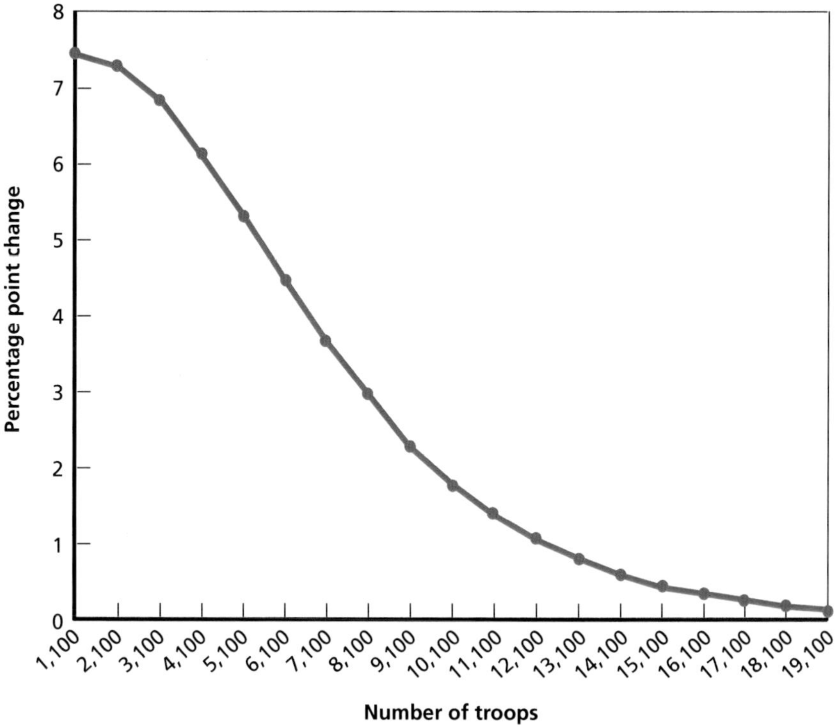

SOURCES: ADC; NSA; Kreutz, 2010; and authors' calculations.

additional 1,000 troops.[14] The estimations demonstrate that the lower end of the troop curve is where the majority of the action takes place in terms of impact. Alternatively stated, there is a clear decreasing marginal return to troop size: Each additional boot on the ground offers less and less by way of improving outcomes.

Finally, Figure 3.4 looks at changes in the predicted probability of a government victory as the sole outcome as the level of maximum troops in a conflict increases in increments of 1,000 soldiers. As the

Figure 3.4
Percentage Point Change in Probability of Government Victory per 1,000-Soldier Increase in Maximum Troops Level

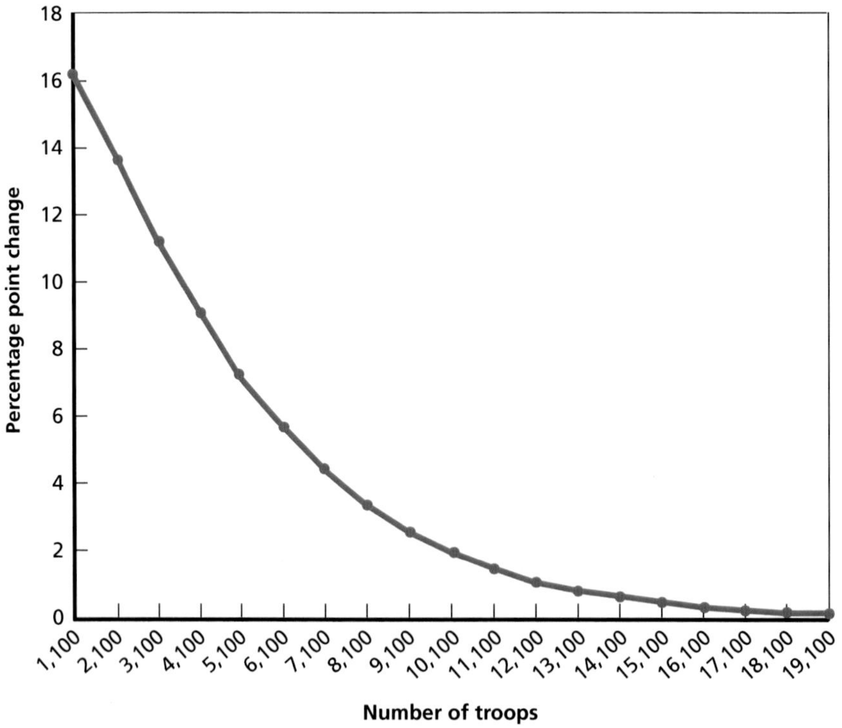

SOURCES: ADC; NSA; Kreutz, 2010; and authors' calculations.

---

[14] For this estimation, we combined both government victory and negotiated settlement into a single outcome.

graphic demonstrates, there are decreasing returns to increased levels of troop deployments in situations where the outcome is a victory by the government. Here again, the biggest outcome "bang for deployment buck" occurs at the lower end of the curve. Of note, out of the 22 cases with U.S. troops present, 81 percent of these cases have troop deployments below 2,000 troops, which represents levels at which ARSOF typically operate. These results are certainly not specific to U.S. SOF or even U.S. forces more generally, but when we restrict modeling efforts to include only U.S. forces, results are similar (albeit with lower levels of statistical significance due to the smaller sample size).

In sum, there is considerable evidence that even small numbers of forces are associated with a partner government's ability to secure a negotiated settlement, even if they seldom help to achieve outright military victory. This broad trend holds even when we focus specifically on cases of small-footprint U.S. military operations (such as those conducted by ARSOF), and it holds even when a great power is providing military assistance to the insurgents. These findings suggest that ARSOF can make an important contribution to great-power competition in cases of active conflict short of conventional interstate wars. Box 3.3 provides additional insights into what FID can and cannot accomplish, using the case of El Salvador.

Unconventional Warfare

UW is an inherently challenging enterprise. Operations are generally conducted by, with, and through local partners or irregular forces, the quality of which varies greatly from country to country. Many movements are highly fractured, riven by internal rivalries. While great powers such as the United States can, with time, improve their training and equipment, imposing a cohesive leadership structure is much more difficult, as suggested by the examples of U.S. support for the mujahideen in Afghanistan and, more recently, various factions in Syria (see Box 3.4 for a discussion of the latter). In contrast, regimes typically begin conflicts with tremendous advantages in organization, resources,

Box 3.3. Support to El Salvador, 1980–1992

Civil war gripped El Salvador between 1980 and 1992, pitting the government and assorted right-wing paramilitary forces against the Farabundo Martí National Liberation Front (FMLN). The United States intervened on the side of the government, providing several billion dollars in military assistance, a few hundred conventional forces, and up to 150 SOF advisors, whose role was to assist in training frontline battalions. That deployment constituted the United States' most protracted and extensive involvement in low-intensity conflict since the Vietnam War.[a]

U.S. advisory support to the government of El Salvador against Communist insurgents in the late Cold War is often held out as a "success story" for small-footprint operations. However, this vignette illustrates both the potential and the limits of such deployments. U.S. support to the government—including the introduction of SOF advisors—helped to prevent the defeat of the regime and ultimately led to a negotiated settlement to El Salvador's civil war, all at relatively low cost. It is worth noting, however, that the war was ultimately ended by the collapse of the Soviet Union, levels of violence remained high following the end of the war, and the United States suffered some reputational costs for supporting a regime implicated in widespread human rights violations.

SOF's Role and Activities

U.S. SOF advisors were tasked with converting the conventionally oriented El Salvador Armed Forces (ESAF) into an effective counterinsurgency force. However, America's light footprint limited its ability to oversee the ESAF's missions, and SOF advisors were prohibited from accompanying the ESAF on patrol, thereby limiting, if not foreclosing, opportunities to enhance interoperability. Finally, despite the ESAF's self-evident difficulties in countering the FMLN, it did not readily accept the advisors' counsel. Over time, the ESAF did shift its approach to countering the FMLN, resulting in the FMLN's abandonment of large-unit operations. However, observers debate the extent to which this change can be directly attributed to the guidance of SOF advisors. The mid-1980s through the early 1990s were largely a struggle of attrition, with neither the government nor the insurgency able to gain a durable military advantage. Developments near the end of the civil war weakened the FMLN significantly and made it more amenable to a negotiated settlement. While most observers agree that U.S. SOF advisors played an important role in building and training an El Salvadoran military that ultimately outlasted the FMLN, the question is whether to adduce this outcome as evidence of U.S. "success."[b]

Box 3.3—continued

Outcomes and Implications

The case of El Salvador illustrates both the benefits and costs of small-footprint support in a conflict environment. On the positive side, a few hundred SOF and conventional force advisors played an important role in blunting and then reversing the FMLN's momentum. Although government forces were never able to defeat the rebels, they were able to weaken them, with the war ending in a negotiated settlement after the collapse of the Soviet Union. SOF deployments thus helped to buy time for the embattled regime in San Salvador.[c] There was a price for these gains in competition, however. The regime and its security forces were responsible for wide-scale human rights abuses, and the United States' reputation suffered by association with the regime. Although the war came to an end, Salvadoran society was polarized and fractured, providing a ripe environment for the rampant criminality that has gripped the country in the post–Cold War period. These dynamics frequently appear in conflict-affected countries. As U.S. decisionmakers grapple with how to pursue competition against Russia and other actors, they must weigh such costs alongside the potential to deny Moscow or others competitive advantage in such regions.

---

[a] Andrew J. Bacevich, *American Military Policy in Small Wars: The Case of El Salvador*, Cambridge, Mass.: Institute for Foreign Policy Analysis, 1988.

[b] Bacevich, 1988; John D. Waghelstein, *Military-to-Military Contacts: Personal Observations—The El Salvador Case*, unpublished draft, Newport, R.I.: U.S. Naval War College, 2002, p. 16; Michael Childress, *The Effectiveness of U.S. Training Efforts in Internal Defense and Development: The Cases of El Salvador and Honduras*, Santa Monica, Calif.: RAND Corporation, MR-250-USDP, 1995, p. 28; Lawrence E. Cline, "The U.S. Advisory Effort in El Salvador," in Kendall D. Gott and Michael G. Brooks, eds., *Security Assistance: U.S. and International Historical Perspectives: The Proceedings of the Combat Studies Institute 2006 Military History Symposium*, Fort Leavenworth, Kan.: Combat Studies Institute Press, 2006, p. 431.

[c] Max G. Manwaring and Court Prisk, "A Strategic View of Insurgencies: Insights from El Salvador," *Small Wars and Insurgencies*, Vol. 4, No. 1, Spring/Summer 1993, p. 64; Walter C. Ladwig, "Influencing Clients in Counterinsurgency: U.S. Involvement in El Salvador's Civil War, 1979–92," *International Security*, Vol. 41, No. 1, Summer 2016, p. 133; Patrick Paterson, *Training Surrogate Forces in International Humanitarian Law: Lessons from Peru, Colombia, El Salvador, and Iraq*, MacDill Air Force Base, Fla.: Joint Special Operations University Press, 2016, p. 75.

Box 3.4. Operations at the Al-Tanf Garrison, 2017–2019

U.S. SOF have operated from Al-Tanf garrison, a remote outpost on the Syrian side of the Syrian-Iraqi-Jordanian border, since the summer of 2016. The strategic importance of Al-Tanf is its proximity to the Syrian M2 highway connecting Damascus to Baghdad.

The U.S. deployment at Al-Tanf is just one dimension of U.S. efforts to contest Iranian influence and deny Russia a total victory in Syria. It serves these aims by disrupting Iran's resupply of militia forces aligned with it in Syria and Lebanon, and by signaling to Damascus and Moscow that the Assad regime will be unable to achieve its main war aim—reestablishing control over its territory from insurgent groups and uninvited foreign interveners (the United States and Turkey)—absent a negotiated process in which Damascus makes concessions to these interveners' interests.[a] In the United States' competition with Russia, U.S. control of Al-Tanf and the territory east of the Euphrates represents a clear U.S. gain, as Syria was a denied environment for the United States prior to the civil war, with Russia the only international power enjoying basing and access inside the country. Today, the United States and its local surrogates are the de facto authority in roughly a third of the country's territory, hold key natural resources (hydrocarbons, water), and control strategic ground lines of communication, such as Al-Tanf.

SOF's Role and Activities

The primary mission of U.S. SOF at Al-Tanf is to train surrogate forces to liberate, hold, and prevent the return of ISIL in territory formerly under the group's control. Open-source reporting indicates that in late 2018, 200 American forces were deployed at Al-Tanf for the training mission. The recipients of the training were Vetted Syrian Opposition (VSO) groups composed of Syrians opposed to ISIL who fled their home governorates when ISIL occupied that territory. A condition of U.S. training was that the recipients commit to fighting ISIL as opposed to the Syrian regime. U.S. SOF were particularly vigilant in monitoring VSO compliance with their pledge, as U.S. legal authorities for the DoD training mission do not extend to fighting the Assad regime, and VSOs that broke their pledge and launched attacks on the regime created force protection issues since the VSOs and U.S. SOF were co-located at Al-Tanf, meaning American personnel would be vulnerable to regime reprisals.[b]

SOF deployments to the Al-Tanf garrison in Syria were not initially intended to be a tool of great-power competition. Over time, however, the goals for this outpost expanded to include efforts to disrupt Iranian support to its proxies in the region and to secure bargaining leverage for the United States in an eventual peace settlement for Syria.[c]

Box 3.4—continued

Outcomes and Implications

The case of the Al-Tanf garrison in Syria suggests that success may be easier to achieve if the United States pursues more modest goals. SOF at Al-Tanf were not pursuing the overthrow of the Assad regime. Rather, alongside their counterterrorism mission, they were operating in a denied environment to disrupt Iranian supply lines to its proxies in the region. In the short term, these efforts appear to have been successful. With the changes to U.S. posture in the region, however, it is unclear how enduring these gains are likely to be. As with security cooperation in fragile states, the Al-Tanf example suggests the critical importance of embedding SOF deployments within a broader, long-term political-military plan. Without such a framework, the use of SOF may buy the United States some time but is unlikely to lead to enduring changes in the competitive environment.

[a] Lolita Baldor, "US General Visits Troops Fighting Islamic State in Syria," Associated Press, October 22, 2018.

[b] Sune Engel Rasmussen and Michael R. Gordon, "A Small U.S. Base Gets in Iran's Way—but Maybe Not for Long," *Wall Street Journal*, December 27, 2018; Mohammed Ersan, "Syrian Rebel Commander: 150 US Troops at Al-Tanf Base," *Al-Monitor*, June 1, 2017; Carla Bab, "US Cuts Ties with Local Syrian Group Trained to Fight IS," *Voice of America*, July 27, 2017.

[c] Baldor 2018; David Botti, "First Came ISIS, Then Iran: How the Mission at a U.S. Base in Syria Kept Growing," *New York Times*, February 14, 2019.

training, and materiel. It is thus unsurprising that prior studies of UW have typically not found high odds of success.[15]

Attempting to evaluate UW with any precision, however, is extremely difficult because these efforts are often clandestine or covert, making it nearly impossible to assemble an accurate and relatively comprehensive dataset. Rather than attempting to develop such a dataset, we have instead relied on the excellent dataset of Cold War–era U.S. efforts to effect regime change compiled by the political scientist Lind-

[15] Seth Jones, *Waging Insurgent Warfare: Lessons from the Viet Cong to the Islamic State*, New York: Oxford University Press, 2017, pp. 164–165; Lindsey A. O'Rourke, *Covert Regime Change: America's Secret Cold War*, Ithaca, N.Y.: Cornell University Press, 2018.

sey O'Rourke.[16] Restricting our analysis to the Cold War era obviously limits our ability to speak to more recent UW efforts. It does, on the other hand, allow us to use relatively comprehensive data to establish a baseline set of expectations. A focus on regime change also clearly limits our ability to assess the effectiveness of UW efforts more broadly. UW can be—and historically often has been—used to overthrow governments. But it has also been used for less ambitious purposes, such as disrupting adversary operations or imposing costs on adversaries. As the vignette in Box 3.4 suggests, these less ambitious goals may be (unsurprisingly) easier to achieve, but their effects may also be more easily reversed as soon as the United States ceases active operations.

O'Rourke's data make clear that, if success is understood in terms of overthrowing a target regime, the odds of success are low and the risks very high. Using a variety of declassified U.S. government documents in addition to secondary sources and interviews, O'Rourke compiled a list of 72 episodes of U.S. efforts at regime change from 1947 to 1989, where regime change was defined as an operation to replace another state's effective political leadership by significantly altering the composition of that state's ruling elite, its administrative apparatus, or its institutional structure. The vast majority of these efforts (66) were covert, and the remainder (6) were overt.[17] Most of the time (72 percent of cases), the United States targeted authoritarian states, but it did target democracies as well.[18] Some of the findings and consequences reported by O'Rourke merit highlighting. Overall, U.S.-backed covert

---

[16] O'Rourke, 2018. We reconstructed the data from tables provided in the book. O'Rourke did not respond to our email request to share the data files.

[17] Covert regime change denotes that the intervening state does not publicly acknowledge its role. This may include assassination attempts of foreign leaders, coup sponsorship, the influence of foreign elections, inciting popular revolution, and supporting dissident or insurgent groups aiming to topple the regime. Overt regime change implies publicly acknowledged operations or attempts to replace the political leadership of a foreign state, including the use of military force (either via war, air strikes, or limited invasions) (O'Rourke, 2018, pp. 14–15).

[18] Regime characteristics of target countries are as follows: 18 democracies, 0 monarchies, 11 personalist regimes, 27 single party states, and 18 military regimes, as defined in Barbara Geddes, Joseph Wright, and Erica Frantz, "Autocratic Breakdown and Regime Transitions: A New Data Set," *Perspectives on Politics*, Vol. 12, No. 2, 2014.

efforts worked just shy of 40 percent of the time. However, O'Rourke found that they were most likely to succeed against democratic governments, weak states, and American allies. Targeting Soviet allies worked just 10 percent of the time. Figure 3.5 displays these differing effects. It shows the success rates of regime change efforts but divides them according to the alignment of the target country: Soviet ally, U.S. ally, and nonaligned. As the graphic makes clear, the United States was highly unlikely to successfully remove leadership in countries aligned with the Soviet Union. Rates of failure in these instances were nearly 90 percent. By contrast, the United States enjoyed its highest success rates and lowest failure rates when it targeted its own allies for regime change. Finally, results were largely mixed when the United States aimed at removing the leadership of nonaligned states. In sum, the

Figure 3.5
Regime Change Rates and Target Country Alignment During the Cold War

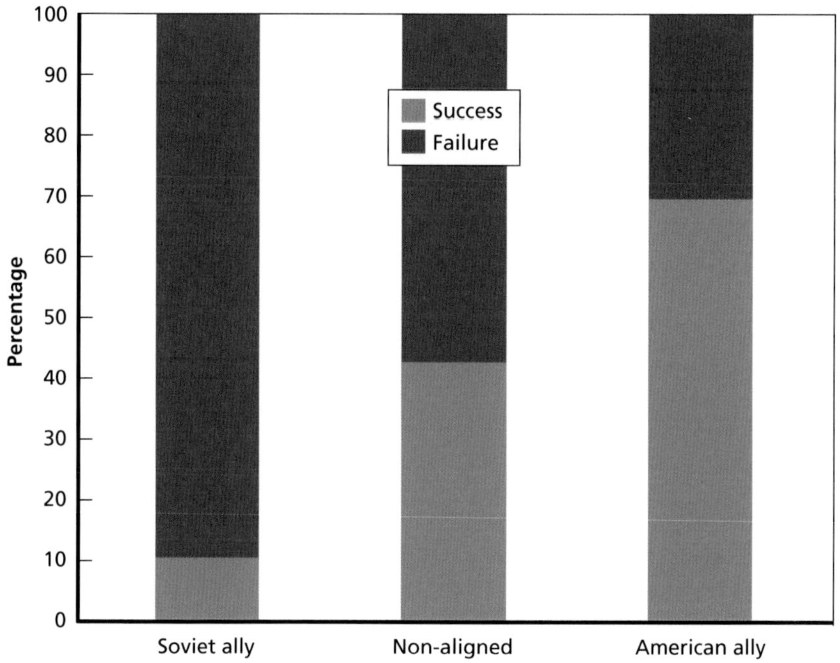

SOURCE: O'Rourke, 2018.

data make clear that unconventional regime change is an effort that is ultimately met with failure more often than success. Success rates in the short term are modest at best.

The longer-term effects of attempting to replace foreign governments were also concerning. O'Rourke found that the United States was more than six times as likely to experience a militarized interstate dispute (MID) with the targeted country in the ten years following the intervention than it was to experience such a dispute with other countries.[19] Moreover, regime change efforts exhibited negative effects on the target states. Countries that the United States overthrew experienced statistically significant declines in levels of democracy. More worryingly, countries where U.S. covert efforts failed were more likely to fall into civil wars within ten years of the intervention. Finally, failed U.S. interventions were also a strong predictor of mass killings in the target country within ten years.[20]

The majority of operations in O'Rourke's dataset were led by the Central Intelligence Agency (CIA). To better understand the effectiveness of SOF in such operations, we merged information on U.S. special warfare operations undertaken since World War II with O'Rourke's data. These data come from a prior RAND effort to catalog and characterize U.S. special warfare campaigns and include 25 cases of UW.[21]

By combining data on U.S.-led regime change efforts and U.S. UW operations, we are able to gauge success rates with and without SOF involvement. Of the 25 UW cases identified, 20 corresponded to regime change efforts classified by O'Rourke. As Figure 3.6 shows, UW efforts led by SOF were successful just under one-third of the time, while UW efforts led by other government agencies were successful in just over one-quarter of the relevant cases. Given the small

---

[19] Failed covert operations were a statistically significant predictor of a MID within ten years.

[20] These summaries come from O'Rourke, 2018, Chapter 4.

[21] Dan Madden, Dick Hoffmann, Michael Johnson, Fred Krawchuk, Bruce R. Nardulli, John E. Peters, Linda Robinson, and Abby Doll, *Toward Operational Art in Special Warfare*, Santa Monica, Calif.: RAND Corporation, RR-779-A, 2016. Data come from Appendix D, "Universe of U.S. Special Warfare Operations."

Figure 3.6
Success Rates of Regime Change Orchestrated via Unconventional Warfare During the Cold War

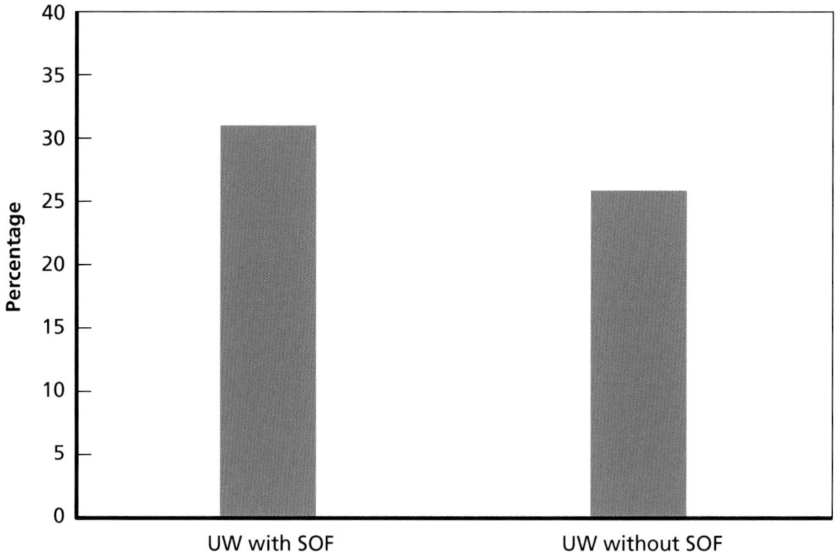

SOURCES: O'Rourke, 2018; Madden et al., 2019.

sample size, however, the difference in these success rates is not statistically significant.

Operations in the Information Environment

OIE can, and do, occur across a range of environments in strategic competition, from the lowest-intensity, steady-state theaters to intensified operations to active war zones. OIE can be powerful when conducted on their own or in conjunction with other ARSOF or conventional activities, such as FID or direct action.

While OIE are executed both by ARSOF and by conventional forces, ARSOF's unique characteristics create certain advantages when considering which entity should lead OIE activities. For example, the highly integrated nature of OIE and the demand for skills such as cultural understanding, foreign language proficiency, and small-footprint approaches relate directly to ARSOF's experience and capabilities.

At the same time, advances in information and communication technology open the possibility for OIE to be used without a physical footprint on the ground in targeted countries. Consequently, it is important to evaluate what OIE can and cannot accomplish apart from other military activities. Such evaluations not only may help us understand the potential effectiveness of U.S. operations but may also give us a better understanding of Russian and other hostile OIE.

As with the other activities we have evaluated in this report, data limitations make it difficult to directly evaluate the direct impact of ARSOF-specific activities. We therefore adopted for an indirect approach. We conducted a systematic review of the academic literature on various forms of political or civic *communication campaigns*, which we define as organized efforts to induce large numbers of people to act on preexisting beliefs (such as by voting or participating in a demonstration), change their beliefs (for instance, by accepting new political views or by abandoning faith in previously held views), or change the manner in which they form beliefs relevant to politics or civic life (such as through media literacy efforts). The term is related to but broader than *public diplomacy*, although it is narrower than the U.S. military's concept of OIE.[22]

Adapting a framework based on International Initiative for Impact Evaluation (3ie) guidelines, we conducted a systematic review of the academic literature on various forms of communication campaigns.[23] In the vast majority of cases, the sources we reviewed employed experiments to rigorously evaluate the effect of a given intervention. These interventions included television advertising, door-to-door canvassing, workshops, or other communication campaigns intended to influence

---

[22] The Joint Chiefs of Staff's *Joint Concept for Operating in the Information Environment* (2018) describes OIE as activities occurring in the information environment, which the Joint Chiefs' *Dictionary of Military and Associated Terms* (2016) defines as "the aggregate of individuals, organizations, and systems that collect, process, disseminate, or act on information."

[23] Caitlin McCulloch and Stephen Watts, *Evaluating the Effectiveness of Public Communication Campaigns and Their Implications for Strategic Competition with Russia*, Santa Monica, Calif.: RAND Corporation, RR-A412-2, 2021.

political behavior. The full details of our analysis can be found in a companion report, *Evaluating the Effectiveness of Public Communication Campaigns and Their Implications for Strategic Competition with Russia*.[24] In this section, we summarize the findings of the companion report, with a focus on four key themes with relevance for ARSOF: face-to-face versus remote messaging, message content, targeting, and competition environment.

The studies covered in our review indicate that the most effective information campaigns, especially for behavioral change (such as an increase in voter turnout) or change in favorability or attitude (such as more-positive attitudes toward the West) are face-to-face, repeated campaigns. In campaigns focused on eliciting electoral turnout, for example, face-to-face campaigns led to increases in voter turnout among groups exposed to the communication campaign that were more than twice as high as the increases resulting from remote campaigns.[25] Repeated contact is especially effective, according to the articles in our review.[26]

In terms of message content, negative and positive messages appear to be almost equally effective in motivating behavioral change, with both increasing turnout by around 3 percent in the studies reviewed.[27] The positive or negative content of messages appears to matter less in shifting voter turnout than other factors, including whether the information campaign was face-to-face or remote and whether it was

---

[24] McCulloch and Watts, 2021.

[25] For two examples of this increased impact, please see David Nickerson, Ryan Friedrichs, and David King. "Partisan Mobilization Campaigns in the Field: Results from a Statewide Turnout Experiment in Michigan," *Political Research Quarterly*, Vol. 59, No. 1, 2006; and Alan Gerber and Donald Green, "The Effects of Canvassing, Telephone Calls, and Direct Mail on Voter Turnout: A Field Experiment," *American Political Science Review*, Vol. 94, No. 3, 2000.

[26] McCulloch and Watts, 2021, but also supported in another meta-analysis of media literacy: Se-Hoon Jeong, Hyunyi Cho, and Yoori Hwang, "Media Literacy Interventions: A Meta-Analytic Review," *Journal of Communication*, Vol. 62, No. 3, 2012.

[27] McCulloch and Watts, 2021, but this variation in impact is also supported in a meta-analysis of negative campaigning: Richard Lau, Lee Sigelman, and Ivy Brown Rovner, "The Effects of Negative Political Campaigns: A Meta-Analytic Reassessment," *Journal of Politics*, Vol. 64, No. 4, 2007.

repeated or a single event. There is some limited evidence to suggest that negative messaging can slightly decrease political participation, likely because of increased skepticism about democratic processes.[28] There is strong evidence indicating that negative messaging can lead to backlash against the actors responsible for those messages if the messages are successfully attributed to the sender.[29] Taken together, these findings suggest that Russia's negative messages about democracy do not have any inherent advantages against Western campaigns designed to reinforce confidence in governance. Indeed, if Western governments can successfully attribute Russia's messaging campaigns to Moscow, these campaigns might be made to work against Russia. Media literacy campaigns may also be helpful. There are some promising early signs that media literacy inoculation might be successful in combating misinformation campaigns or biased media,[30] and there is limited evidence that media literacy inoculation is more successful than after-the-fact correction of misinformation, because repetition may reinforce the misinformation.[31]

Targeting greatly increases the success rate of interventions, especially targeting that stresses peer groups or community norms.[32] For

---

[28] Jesse Driscoll and F. Daniel Hidalgo, "Intended and Unintended Consequences of Democracy Promotion Assistant to Georgia After the Rose Revolution," *Research and Politics*, Vol. 1, No. 1, 2014.

[29] Lau, Sigelman, and Rovner, 2007.

[30] Srividya Ramasubramanian, "Media-Based Strategies to Reduce Racial Stereotypes Activated by News Stories," *Journalism and Mass Communication Quarterly*, Vol. 84, No. 2, 2007; Melissa Tully, Emily Vraga, and Leticia Bode, "Designing and Testing News Literacy Messages for Social Media," *Mass Communication and Society*, Vol. 23, No. 1, 2020; Emily Vraga and Melissa Tully, "Media Literacy Messages and Hostile Media Perceptions: Processing of Nonpartisan Versus Partisan Political Information," *Mass Communication and Society*, Vol. 18, No. 4, 2015.

[31] Adam Berinsky, "Rumors and Health Care Reform: Experiments in Political Misinformation," *British Journal of Political Science*, Vol. 47, No. 2, 2017.

[32] For one example, see Alan Gerber, Dan Green, and Christopher Larimer, "Social Pressure and Voter Turnout: Evidence from a Large-Scale Field Experiment," *American Political Science Review*, Vol. 102, No. 1, 2008. Overall, in the data in McCulloch and Watts, 2021, get-out-the-vote mail campaigns that personalized their messages to individual and neighborhood voting history were successful in increasing electoral turnout by an average of

example, mail campaigns that used social pressure increased voter turnout, on average, by nearly three times more than the increase in voter turnout from other mail campaigns.

Although our systematic review provides evidence of the effect of information campaigns, we note that the effect sizes for messaging campaigns—especially remote and less intensive ones—tend to be small and tend to persuade primarily those who do not have strong preexisting beliefs. A study that directly evaluated Russian messaging campaigns found results consistent with our review of the broader field. Political scientists Leonid Peisakhin and Arturas Rozenas found that exposure to Russian television among Ukrainian populations had only very small effects on voting behavior and political views. Populations in range of Russian television broadcasts differed in their voting behavior and their opinion of their own and the Russian government by less than a percentage point from populations that did not receive such broadcasts, despite the popularity of Russian television and the heavily slanted political content of the television programming.[33]

However, even small effect sizes may be decisive in closely contested elections in majoritarian electoral systems, such as those in the United States. They may also be important in revolutionary situations, such as in Poland during much of the 1980s (see Box 3.5), when opinions are more fluid. In other environments, however, they may make little difference for a target country's broad trajectory (although they may have larger effects within certain subpopulations). For example, the overall effectiveness of OIE undertaken by ARSOF in the Balkans over the past two decades has been mixed (see Box 3.6).

Perhaps most important for our focus on competition, our literature survey found moderate evidence that, in "saturated" media environments, in which people are bombarded by a wide range of messages, adversarial messaging efforts tend to cancel each other out. This finding held true in both the electoral literature, focused on competing

---

4.67 percent, while similar but untargeted get-out-the-vote mail campaigns increased electoral turnout by an average of 1.75 percent.

[33] Leonid Peisakhin and Arturas Rozenas, "Electoral Effects of Biased Media: Russian Television in Ukraine," *American Journal of Political Science*, Vol. 62, No. 3, 2018.

Box 3.5. Poland's Solidarity Movement and Covert U.S. Operations in the Information Environment

The case of CIA support to the Polish Solidarity Movement throughout the 1980s represents one of the extremely few publicly known cases of covert OIE by the U.S. government. Codenamed QRHELPFUL, the CIA's operation to furtively assist a protest movement initiated by the trade union Solidarity in Poland provides lessons for conducting offensive influence activity against a near-peer competitor. Although ARSOF did not play a role, the case offers important insights applicable to special operations. Perhaps most remarkably, the CIA was able to support Solidarity while largely concealing its hand from attribution, relying on a vast and diverse network through which it provided material assistance to Polish sources conducting messaging.[a]

The CIA's Role and Activities

U.S. policy toward Solidarity, which formed in late 1980, was initially reactive. But shortly after the declaration of martial law in late 1981, President Ronald Reagan initiated QRHELPFUL, an operation to provide money, printing capabilities, and equipment for radio and TV broadcasts to members of the by-then underground Solidarity Movement. Roughly three weeks after signing a secret directive that authorized covert measures to "neutralize the efforts of the U.S.S.R.," Reagan met with Pope John Paul II in mid-1982, and the two discussed an effort to bring down the Soviet Union through what Reagan's then–National Security Advisor Richard Allen called "one of the great secret alliances of all time."[b] Between then and 1989, when Solidarity again became legal and ousted ruling Communists through democratic elections, the U.S. intelligence community and the Catholic Church funneled tons of printing and broadcasting equipment, computers, and telex machines to Solidarity operatives, often with the help of European labor organizations, the American Federation of Labor and Congress of Industrial Organizations, and the National Endowment for Democracy.[c]

Outcomes and Implications

QRHELPFUL illustrates several themes regarding effective communications campaigns. First, while the CIA's operation appears to have helped Solidarity, the context for this operation was critical to its success. In particular, had the Soviet Union not been seeking opportunities for civil society participation, it is unlikely that the local networks through which the CIA was operating could have survived. Second, the existence of large, capable partners on the ground was critical. The operation utilized a vast network of agents and actors, ranging from Catholic priests to West European socialists, all of whom worked toward a common goal while providing distinct forms of support. The CIA did not attempt to develop IO themes itself or conduct the OIE campaign; rather, it sought to build the capabilities of already

Box 3.5—continued

highly capable, highly motivated partners. In this sense, probably the most significant factor in the success of QRHELPFUL was the CIA's willingness to act as a "middleman," using intelligence expertise to provide operational security while not presuming Agency-knows-best regarding propaganda production and dissemination.

QRHELPFUL also relied on preexisting trends to benefit its activities, such as widespread Polish antipathy for Communist governance, strong support for the church, and a robust labor movement that could serve as a vanguard for change. In addition, senior U.S. officials—including Reagan—and Solidarity leadership both recognized the importance of targeting subpopulations and leveraging community groups, such as the church, in garnering support for the movement.

Digital communications play an exponentially larger role in modern OIE in Europe than they did during the Cold War. ARSOF has organic intelligence and cultural expertise, but little-to-no independent cyber operations capacity. Contemporary OIE thus involves a wider range of partners with varying capabilities, such as Cyber Command, and requires more intra- and interdepartmental coordination than the Solidarity effort. ARSOF's comparative advantage in working with human networks, gained through past counterterrorism and counterinsurgency operations, could help them in leveraging allies' and partners' expertise in digital networks.

---

[a] Seth Jones, *A Covert Action: Reagan, the CIA, and the Cold War Struggle in Poland*, New York: W.W. Norton & Company, 2018.

[b] Carl Bernstein, "Cover Story: The Holy Alliance," *TIME*, June 24, 2001.

[c] Bernstein, 2001.

political campaigns, and the media literacy literature, focused on the interplay between misleading or "fake" news and factual correction. This finding may have important implications for great-power competition in which OIE plays a major role. In one study, increased Democratic campaign advertising alone was found to shift the probability of someone voting for the Democrats considerably (from a 29 percent chance to a 39 percent chance), while increased Republican campaign advertising alone could shift the probability of someone voting for the Democrats in the other direction (from a 29 percent chance to a

Box 3.6. U.S. Military Operations in the Information Environment in the Balkans, 1992–2017

The U.S. military's experience in the former Yugoslavia following the disintegration of that state in the early 1990s until 2017 provides an extended view into OIE in a distinctly crisis-riven, European setting. Throughout the course of U.S. and NATO intervention in the Balkans, U.S. Army and Air Force SOF played a significant role in enabling OIE, often partnering with U.S. government, allied, and nongovernment parties to facilitate these operations. Several of these operations highlight the challenges facing OIE in this or similar theaters, whereas others illustrate successful means of influencing target audiences. The case of U.S. OIE in the Balkans also demonstrates how the evolution of digital mass communications shaped the effectiveness of influence efforts and provides lessons for operating in a theater that is—in terms of OIE—closely contested by Russia.

ARSOF's Role and Activities

ARSOF inaugurated OIE in the Balkans during humanitarian efforts in Bosnia in the early 1990s. In February 1993, approximately 600,000 leaflets accompanied airdrops of food and medical supplies bound for eastern Bosnia-Herzegovina, targeting mostly isolated Muslim communities. Initial OIE efforts were marred by several oversights and mistakes, including leaflet drops that missed their targets, poor-quality printing, and use of an American flag on leaflets designed to support a multilateral operation.[a]

Beginning in the late 1990s, U.S. Army OIE specialists implemented a three-part "information campaign" that included a public information campaign to establish NATO credibility with international media, a PSYOP campaign to shape local opinions in favor of peacekeepers, and a civil-military cooperation campaign to provide factual information about civil-military relations between coalition forces and local government.[b] With the onset of Operation Allied Force in 1999, OIE became far more focused on directly supporting combat operations. The U.S. Air Force leaned on the 193rd Special Operations Wing to launch radio and television broadcasts from an airborne platform, while the U.S. Army's 4th PSYOP Group launched a multifaceted campaign that included posters, radio and television broadcasts, leaflets, and handbills. During Allied Force, the U.S. dropped more than 104 million leaflets over Kosovo, and more than 2 million leaflets over northern Yugoslavia.[c]

As of mid-2016, the 6th Military Information Support Battalion supported U.S. and allied OIE efforts in Europe, including the Balkans, with more-advanced capabilities, such as social media exploitation and electronic messaging. Operations conducted by U.S. Army special operations civil affairs units in the Balkans show an advanced approach to supporting OIE and humanitarian missions. In 2015, the Civil Military

Box 3.6—continued

Support Element in Bosnia-Herzegovina worked closely with a broad array of U.S. and host-nation partners to promote ethnic inclusivity, assist social programs, and encourage economic development, and their effectiveness was bolstered by their ability to integrate into Bosnia and Herzegovina.[d]

Outcomes and Implications

Overall, OIE in the Balkans undertaken by ARSOF over the past two decades can best be described as mixed success. ARSOF OIE specialists were able to directly support combat and humanitarian operations during regional crises, in part because of their mobility and their ability to sustain OIE operations through internal capabilities, such as Fort Bragg–based printing presses and televised broadcasts. Additionally, ARSOF's experience in the Balkans demonstrates consistent evolution in OIE means, ranging from the black-and-white leaflets used during the initial humanitarian operations to the social media platforms used to support contemporary operations. Over time, command-and-control and the ability of ARSOF specialists to integrate with external U.S. or NATO elements very likely improved. ARSOF also maintains the regional expertise needed to better understand target audiences and cultural sensitivities.

To some extent, ARSOF's effectiveness in OIE as it relates to more-sophisticated adversaries probably hinges on ARSOF operators' ability to integrate with other military and government authorities in theater, including U.S. ambassadors, and other organizations, such as USAID and NGOs.

[a] SGM Herbert A. Friedman (Ret.), "PSYOP Against Milosevic's Yugoslavia," Psywar.org, January 1, 2007; Peter Maass, "3 U.S. Planes Begin Bosnian Relief Effort," *Washington Post*, March 1, 1993.

[b] Friedman, 2007.

[c] Friedman 2007; Ed Rouse, "Psychological Operations & Operation Allied Forces," Psywarrior.com, undated; Tom Bowman, "National Guard Plane 'Shoots' Message at Yugoslav Audience; U.S. Perspective on War, Rebuttal of Milosevic," *Baltimore Sun*, June 5, 1999.

[d] Captain Nick Israel and Captain Albert Finochiarro, "6th MISB(A)'s Essential Role in the SOCEUR AOR," *Special Warfare*, Vol. 29, No. 1, January–June 2016; Janice Burton, "CMSE BiH," *Special Warfare*, Vol. 29, No. 1, January–June 2016.

17.5 percent chance).[34] However, this study found that, if both campaigns have saturated a market with advertisements, voting changes little from the mean, and audience predisposition to a particular party is much more important in predicting voting for a particular party. These findings have a clear analogue in the United States' competition with Russia. Previous RAND work has noted the "firehose" of Russian misinformation and its impacts, and the authors suggest that the way to combat the impact of a flood of fake stories may be a countervailing flood in the opposite direction.[35]

Studies of electoral politics suggest that, if the United States commits to large-scale and well-targeted counter-messaging, it may be able to neutralize Russia's efforts in the information or cognitive environment. Indeed, when "playing defense" (i.e., conducting counter-messaging in among allies and close partners), the United States may have considerable advantages. First, it begins with a much more positive image than Russia among most of its allies and partners and indeed most countries globally. Second, the United States has better on-the-ground access in these countries, enabling it much more freedom when seeking to target its messages and work through local actors.

Taken together, the studies in our systematic review have three important implications for understanding the threat posed by Russian OIE, potential U.S. responses, and the value of ARSOF contributions to these operations. First, given that the effect of messaging campaigns was typically small, the studies in our sample should help to bound expectations about what can be achieved through OIE, while at the same time also helping to bound our estimates of the threat posed by Russian efforts. Second, the research suggests the importance of defensive OIE efforts since, in more competitive environments, communications efforts often largely cancel each other out. Defensive OIE also benefits from greater ease of organizing face-to-face campaigns (including media literacy education in schools, canvassing for elections,

---

[34] Michael Franz and Travis Rideout, "Does Political Advertising Persuade?" *Political Behavior*, Vol. 29, No. 4, 2007.

[35] Christopher Paul and Miriam Matthews, *The Russian "Firehose of Falsehood" Propaganda Model*, Santa Monica, Calif: RAND Corporation, PE-198-OSD, 2016.

and so on). Third, there are several approaches for making OIE campaigns stronger, including targeting messages to subpopulations and picking target audiences carefully.

Many of the findings in our review suggest that ARSOF might make important and in some cases unique contributions to OIE efforts. For example, ARSOF work closely with local partners, which can help facilitate operations with surrogates who can conduct face-to-face activities and whose familiarity with local environments and frequent presence in theater may help to better target messages to specific subpopulations. OIE is possible without a physical presence, as recent Russian social media campaigns make clear, but our review suggests that physical presence does offer a number of advantages in the conduct of OIE.

CHAPTER FOUR

Conclusion and Policy Recommendations

The U.S. military has made a clear shift in its strategic prioritization of threats. After many years of counterinsurgency and counterterrorism efforts, the threats from peer and near-peer competitors rank at the top. Concepts and doctrine for understanding this strategic competition and the appropriate tools with which to engage in it, however, remain underdeveloped.

This report has sought to improve understanding of the potential for special operations—and particularly ARSOF—as a tool for conducting strategic competition. Because Russia is commonly understood as the Army's "pacing threat" in the near-term future, this report focused on competition with Russia. Our statistical analyses and several of the case studies we used in evaluating the potential effectiveness of ARSOF, however, are not specific to Russia, suggesting that some of the measures we reviewed may have similar utility in other contexts. Many of these findings are also likely relevant to other services' SOF, although these were outside of the scope of this report. In this chapter, we take stock of our findings and present the policy implications that derive from them.

Conclusions

In steady-state environments, U.S. policymakers typically adopt lower-risk, lower-cost approaches to competition. In this context, ARSOF's focus on working through local partners presents clear advantages. ARSOF present low-visibility and light footprint options to develop partner nations' militaries, improve their civil-military relations, help them to plan and implement OIE campaigns, work with them to acquire information on (and ultimately expose and/or disrupt) adversarial networks, and related activities. Moreover, because ARSOF are permitted different authorities than conventional forces, they can generally operate more efficiently across a greater range of activities than conventional forces.

There is substantial evidence to suggest that military partnering activities can not only build the tactical military capabilities of partner nations but also make them more resilient to instability or political subversion by hostile actors. As our case study of ARSOF activities in the Baltics suggests, ARSOF can also help build partner capabilities for resisting foreign invasion and occupation, thus potentially increasing deterrence.

Some of the more direct roles of ARSOF in these environments, such as potentially gathering or helping to fuse and analyze intelligence on competitor or adversary networks, are more difficult to evaluate, especially in unclassified publications. For these roles, too, ARSOF has a number of advantages related to their low-profile activities and their experience with similar missions in other contexts (such as during counterterrorism operations).

There are also, however, a number of limitations or risks associated with ARSOF activities in these environments. Precisely because ARSOF are highly mobile and typically operate in a low-profile manner, they may send less of a deterrent signal than larger, heavier forces that clearly indicate U.S. commitment to protecting the countries and regions in which they are stationed or deployed. Working through partners also inevitably means that the success of U.S. policies will be at least in substantial measure contingent on the behavior of those partners. Less well-governed and less-developed countries have often encountered challenges sustaining the capabilities that U.S. forces have helped them to develop, and they sometimes use those capabilities in ways or for purposes antithetical to U.S. policy.

In intensely competitive environments, such as regions of active conflict, ARSOF also offer key tools. This report has focused particularly on FID and UW. The advantages of ARSOF in this type of environment are not dissimilar to those in lower-risk environments. ARSOF provide an agile, highly independent, small-footprint force highly conducive to low-visibility activities. These characteristics are particularly advantageous in denied environments. Through statistical analyses of prior instances of FID and UW, we identified a number of broad patterns in these types of operations. Foreign support of embattled partner governments, such as the FID operations conducted by ARSOF, has historically greatly improved the chances of the partner government obtaining at least a minimally acceptable outcome, such as a negotiated settlement with insurgents. In contrast, the United States has had much lower rates of success when attempting to overthrow an adversary regime, such as through UW operations. Moreover, UW runs a high risk of unintended consequences, such as escalation to interstate conflict. The example of Syria, however, suggests that less-ambitious uses of UW instruments—such as efforts to disrupt adversary networks in denied environments—may be much more feasible within acceptable levels of risk.

Finally, ARSOF have important roles in the information environment, whether in areas of active conflict or more stable contexts. While capabilities for OIE are by no means unique to ARSOF, ARSOF are an important component of the United States' overall toolkit for contesting Russia's efforts to influence U.S. allies and partners and potentially for pressing U.S. messages further afield in countries closely aligned with Russia (or other competitors). ARSOF's ability to operate on the ground, even in denied or otherwise challenging environments, is potentially useful both for targeting efforts and for recruiting local surrogates. Evidence suggests that these local surrogates are likely to have a number of advantages over remote operations, including intimate local knowledge, ability to engage in face-to-face persuasion, and networks among key subpopulations.

Amid all of the media attention to "information warfare" and particularly vivid events, it is important to examine carefully what the evidence suggests OIE can and cannot do. Rigorous studies of the effects of Russian television propaganda in the former Soviet states of Ukraine and Kyrgyzstan, for instance, found small effect sizes from even extremely high levels of exposure to Russian messaging, and even these effects were concentrated among certain subpopulations. Looking more broadly to rigorous evaluations of political campaigning, voter education initiatives, and so on, we again find a similar picture. OIE and other efforts at political persuasion can nudge public opinion, but normally only by relatively modest amounts. Vigorous countermessaging can further dampen the effect sizes.

Under the right circumstances, these tools can have important effects. In tightly contested elections in electoral systems like the United States' or in potentially revolutionary situations like that in late-Communist Poland, small initial effects from OIE can sometimes have outsized impact—especially if they are not countered through an equally committed response. But it would be dangerous to assume that these instances of outsized impact are representative of the broader potential of OIE.

Table 4.1 provides a summary of potential U.S. goals in competition and the advantages and limitations of ARSOF in achieving them.

Policy Recommendations

The primary purpose of this report is to provide a high-level overview of requirements for competition with Russia, the full range of ways in which ARSOF could improve the U.S. position in this competition, and rigorous evidence of the impact of special operations in the competition space. Based on the insights from our analysis of these topics, we conclude with broader recommendations about how best to realize the value of ARSOF in strategic competition and better integrate these forces into the Army's and DoD's future thinking on competition. These recommendations are intended primarily for DoD, but some require consensus across multiple agencies of the U.S. government.

The Army should revise future iterations of its MDO concept and other formal publications to provide more-concrete guidance for competition and the employment of ARSOF

The overwhelming majority of the Army's current MDO concept is dedicated to conventional warfighting. On the one hand, such an emphasis is entirely understandable: The Army's primary mission is to

Table 4.1
Summary of ARSOF Strengths and Limitations in Strategic Competition

Potential U.S. Goals	ARSOF Strengths	ARSOF Risks and Limitations
• Mitigate adversarial messaging efforts • Engage key populations • Support decisionmakers against influence efforts by malign actors • Improve resilience of partner institutions • Assure foreign partners of U.S. resolve • Deter adversaries • Illuminate and disrupt adversary networks	• Ability to enhance partners' capabilities (for internal resilience and external deterrence) through low cost, persistent presence • Capabilities for low-visibility roles, including in tracking adversary activity and preparations for higher-intensity contingencies • Ability to effectively counter violent activities by surrogates • Ability to disrupt adversary networks in contested environments • Some ability to threaten adversary governments through UW • Ability to enhance effectiveness of OIE through on-the-ground message targeting and recruitment of surrogates	• Challenges in developing sustainable capabilities in partners with poor political, economic development • Risk of misuse of capabilities developed in partners • Limitations in deterrent signal of ARSOF • High risk of failure when directly targeting adversary governments through UW (outside of foreign occupations) • Overall impact of OIE highly contingent on circumstances

win the nation's wars, and it and the other services are the only parts of the U.S. government capable of warfighting. On the other hand, when the competition phase is presented as being of co-equal importance to the conflict phase but the large majority of attention and conceptual innovations concern warfighting, there are clearly opportunities for improvement. Considering that Russian military thinking suggests that conventional military activities are only a small contributor to the realization of a country's strategic goals in the current environment, it is important that future iterations of the MDO concept and other U.S. military concepts, strategies, and doctrine more generally treat the irregular aspects of competition extensively.

Fully outlining such formal guidance is beyond the scope of this study. A comparison of the current MDO concept with the ARSOF roles outlined in this report, however, indicates what several of the elements of a revised MDO concept for competition might include. In its current iteration, the MDO concept has three main pillars for the competition space:

1. Enable defeat of information and unconventional warfare.
2. Conduct intelligence and counter adversary reconnaissance.
3. Demonstrate credible deterrent.

Regarding the requirement to conduct intelligence and counter adversary reconnaissance, there are clear limitations on what can be discussed in an unclassified document. Consequently, there may be little that can be done in publicly available military concepts and doctrine to provide more insight into how ARSOF and other elements of the Joint Force can support this requirement.

In the case of demonstrating a credible deterrent, however, there are clear opportunities to expand and deepen the discussion. Deterrence encompasses unconventional and irregular elements, as well as conventional ones. The case study of ARSOF activities in the Baltics suggests that the United States might enhance deterrence in part by raising the costs of invasion and occupation through the preventive creation of a UW capability in U.S. allies and partners. Similarly, adversaries might be deterred from efforts to destabilize or subvert U.S. allies and partners if the United States enhanced their ability to conduct irregular warfare.

The greatest opportunities to add depth are in the MDO concept's discussion of information warfare and unconventional warfare.

First, a much broader discussion of OIE is warranted. The current iteration of the MDO concept states that the "Army primarily contributes to the strategic narrative . . . by reinforcing the resolve and commitment of the U.S. to its partner and demonstrating its capabilities as a credible deterrent."[1] Much of the discussion focuses on the enablers

---

1 TRADOC, 2018, p. 29.

of information warfare, such as "access to intelligence, cyberspace, and EMS [emergency medical service] capabilities" and broader authorities, rather than on what the Army or Joint Force commander would do with those capabilities.[2] Other topics that merit discussion include the ways in which ARSOF and other elements of the U.S. military might work with partner forces to develop their capabilities for OIE or to enhance the resilience of partner forces to adversary messaging or other influence attempts. Other key topics for future iterations of the Army's MDO concept include opportunities to work with local partners, such as nongovernmental organizations, when appropriate authorities and permissions exist, and a discussion of how civil affairs units might work with partners to provide government services to vulnerable subpopulations who might be targeted for adversary messaging.

There is also a need to expand on how Army forces should carry out indirect and direct roles in irregular warfare. The MDO concept is absolutely correct in declaring, "When an adversary employs proxies, Army forces defeat them principally through the indirect enabling of partners, but can support directly through unilateral action."[3] But in contrast to the pages of discussion for how MDO is to be waged in conventional combat, no further explanation of the indirect enabling of partners is provided. Related topics requiring expanded treatment include FID principles and the potential to integrate nonlethal activities, such as CAO, with lethal ones; the importance of persistent presence and building relationships long before a conflict breaks out and remaining engaged long after (points that our review of the quantitative literature and our case studies of the CTS in Iraq and the U.S. advisory mission in El Salvador suggest are critical); and the challenges posed by poorly governed partners. Our analysis suggests that poor governance has important implications for interagency cooperation and for the need for a fusion of advisory roles for both ARSOF and conventional forces.

There is also a need for greater discussion of more-aggressive or more-offensive operations. This includes how ARSOF or other ele-

---

2 TRADOC, 2018, p. 29.

3 TRADOC, 2018, p. 28.

ments of the Joint Force might conduct OIE in countries not aligned with the United States, and how ARSOF might be employed in denied environments to disrupt adversary networks or even weaken adversary governments.

Obviously, no single document can fully cover the complexity of the competition space. But without at least reference to many of these key issues, there is a risk that concepts will be built and resources allocated without incorporating the underlying requirements of successful competition against irregular threats.

U.S. Special Operations Command and U.S. Army Special Operations Command should periodically review allocations of ARSOF against the evidence of utility in strategic competition to ensure optimal employment

ARSOF are a low-density part of the Joint Force. For years, they have had trouble keeping pace with the extraordinarily high demand of counterterrorism missions. Despite the NDS's focus on great-power competition, terrorist threats will not disappear; they remain the fifth-ranked priority in the NDS. ARSOF possess unique capabilities that make them high-demand forces for counterterrorism, but the same can be said of missions in the competition space.

Efforts are currently ongoing to examine how SOF might be reallocated in light of current needs.[4] The discussions of ARSOF effectiveness in this report can be used to inform these and future analyses of ARSOF allocation. The evidence suggests that ARSOF can make major contributions to strategic competition. ARSOF can help to build durable capacity among allies and partners in the right contexts (especially when ARSOF maintains a persistent presence), can help to defeat armed proxies targeting allied or partner governments (usually with a

---

[4] The Fiscal Year 2020 National Defense Authorization Act (Pub L. 116-92) directed an independent assessment of special operations force structure. Further, USSOCOM released a Special Operations Forces Culture and Ethics Comprehensive Review in January 2020 that recommends an internal review of SOF employment. While both of these reviews will likely be completed prior to publication of this report, the authors believe the findings in this report could help inform future analyses.

relatively small footprint), and can facilitate a number of practices identified with successful OIE.

The Office of the Secretary of Defense and the combatant commands should consider the use of ARSOF for cost-imposing strategies against Russia only in relatively rare circumstances

Russia has had to pay some economic cost for its more-aggressive foreign policies since 2014, but thus far, Russia appears to be able to bear these costs indefinitely. This situation has prompted many U.S. and other Western observers to call for imposing higher costs on Russia for its malign activities. ARSOF offer some options for imposing such costs on Moscow through their capabilities for UW and offensive OIE. Before committing to the use of such capabilities, however, senior decisionmakers must carefully weigh the expected utility of these options.

Our analysis suggests that defenders enjoy advantages in terms of the expected effectiveness of different types of operations:

- **FID:** Statistical analyses suggest that FID activities are often successful in securing at least minimally acceptable outcomes to civil conflicts in allies and partners, even with relatively small commitments of U.S. forces. This finding suggests that there are clear limits to what Russia can accomplish through the use of proxies to instigate civil wars or other violent conflicts, at least when the United States provides military support to the targeted government.
- **UW:** At least when the aim is to overthrow adversary governments or governments allied with U.S. adversaries, UW has relatively low success rates. It may be more successful when used for less ambitious goals, such as disrupting adversary lines of communication in denied environments where reasonably effective and politically acceptable local surrogates exist. But the vignette on the Al-Tanf garrison also suggests that such incremental gains are highly sensitive to broader changes outside ARSOF control. In favorable circumstances, ARSOF might be employed to impose costs on Russia or Russian partner governments through UW, but historical rates of success suggest that a high degree of caution is warranted in such offensive operations.

- **OIE:** The record of OIE is less clear, although here, too, defenders enjoy a number of advantages, including better understanding of audiences for the targeting of message campaigns, much greater ability to conduct face-to-face messaging campaigns, and so on.

In terms of effectiveness, our analyses suggest that defending governments enjoy many advantages over states that use irregular warfare offensively. In terms of costs, however, the equation may be flipped. Open-source analyses of offensive uses of OIE (such as misinformation designed to influence electoral outcomes) and UW suggest that such operations are relatively inexpensive.[5] Consequently, a government that is willing to accept numerous inexpensive failures may be able to successfully impose costs on an adversary that is forced to defend against these probes.

Russia clearly seems willing to engage in many such offensive operations, even if it results in diplomatic isolation, economic sanctions, and other adverse consequences.[6] It is less clear that such offensive irregular operations would be in the United States' national interest. For one thing, the United States enjoys a very different position in the international system; with its vast economic relations and large number of allies and partners, it has a much greater stake in stability than Russia. For another, the United States has many competitive advantages over Russia, including economic sanctions and other economic instruments, which are readily available to U.S. decisionmakers.[7] The United States, in short, does not need to engage in offensive

---

[5] For instance, according to the U.S. indictment against Russian individuals associated with the Internet Research Agency, Russia was spending approximately $1.25 million per month on internet-based efforts to influence the U.S. elections in 2016 (*United States of America v. Internet Research Agency LLC* et al., 18 U.S.C. §§ 2, 371, 1349, 10281A).

[6] For a broader discussion, see Sean M. Zeigler, Dara Massicot, Elina Treyger, Naoko Aoki, Chandler Sachs, and Stephen Watts, *Analysis of Russian Irregular Threats*, Santa Monica, Calif.: RAND Corporation, RR-A412-3, 2021.

[7] James Dobbins, Raphael S. Cohen, Nathan Chandler, Bryan Frederick, Edward Geist, Paul DeLuca, Forrest E. Morgan, Howard J. Shatz, and Brent Williams, *Extending Russia: Competing from Advantageous Ground*, Santa Monica, Calif.: RAND Corporation, RR-3063-A, 2019.

irregular operations with relatively low odds of success and high risks in order to impose costs on Russia. In many cases, the most effective use of ARSOF will be in defensive operations, such as FID designed to protect key allies or partners.

There may well be specific contexts in which UW and aggressive uses of OIE are appropriate tools for the United States to compel Russia to cease certain activities or to disrupt and degrade its ability to pursue them. But the potential benefits of such instruments must be carefully weighed against the costs, risks, and likelihood of success. The U.S. record of overthrowing hostile governments during the Cold War and, more recently, the complicated dynamics of its deployments in eastern Syria suggest that such options should be employed only when there are extremely strong grounds for believing that the odds of success are considerably better than their historical baseline or there are no other reasonable alternatives for achieving a high-priority goal.

The Office of the Secretary of Defense and other key stakeholders should embed special operations in a broader, long-term political-military strategy

Special operations are seldom decisive by themselves. Conventional ground forces offer the potential to seize and hold territory, but usually at enormous cost. Special operations, in contrast, can nudge local dynamics in directions favorable to U.S. interests at low cost—that is, they offer "the ability to influence partners, populations, and threats toward achievement of our regional or strategic objectives [including by] retaining decision space, maximizing desirable strategic options, or . . . denying an adversary a decisive positional advantage."[8]

The strategic gains realized through all acts of warfare are easily squandered if they are not embedded in a broader political-military strategy—a truism since the times of Clausewitz, and one that was reinforced by the U.S. experience in Iraq. But this broader maxim is particularly true of special operations, where gains tend to be incremental and are realized through local partners with their own objectives.

---

[8] Votel et al., 2016, p. 108.

The evidence in this report provides many examples of gains being either lost or at least narrowly limited through either a failure of strategic vision or a failure of commitment. UW campaigns launched by the United States in the late Cold War in places such as El Salvador, for instance, were successful in their narrow objectives, but the fragility of the postconflict states left them vulnerable to a new set of problems as soon as their wars ended. In the case of the U.S. garrison at Al-Tanf in Syria, the United States succeeded in disrupting an Iranian "land bridge" to its regional proxy network, but the lack of long-term commitment risks making these gains short-lived. The quantitative evidence presented in this and other studies suggests that these are not isolated incidents. As we discussed in the section on the effectiveness of security cooperation in Chapter Three, for instance, such activities in less developed, poorly governed states generally yield gains that cannot be sustained unless embedded within a long-term, broader political-military effort.

Just as DoD and the rest of the U.S. government should strive to embed special operations within a broader, long-term political-military strategy, ARSOF must ensure that their activities are similarly synchronized with other interagency actors. In particular, ARSOF should continue to form and maintain strong relationships with U.S. ambassadors and country teams. At the same time, interagency actors and conventional military organizations should endeavor to integrate ARSOF equities and contributions as a matter of routine throughout their planning and strategic development processes. Such efforts must occur among multiple organizations from the tactical through the strategic levels and should consider ARSOF as an integral component of overall planning, rather than a separate and distinct supporting element.

Final Thoughts

Strategic competition is an extraordinarily complex challenge, combining military, diplomatic, information, and economic instruments in myriad and often unexpected ways. The evidence of this report suggests that ARSOF are an important tool that could be better utilized to confront the threats posed by Russia and other revisionist competitors.

APPENDIX

Technical Discussion of Statistical Modeling of FID

In this appendix, we provide more details of our statistical modeling of the effectiveness of FID, including information on our data and modeling approach.

Data and Intervention Cases

Our analysis covers 250 episodes of violent conflict from 1946 through 2014, drawing from the Uppsala Conflict Data Program—Peace Research Institute Oslo (UCDP-PRIO) Armed Conflict Dataset (ACD). In the ACD, conflict is defined as "a contest incompatibility that concerns government and/or territory . . . of which at least one [party] is the government of a state."[1] We limited our analysis to conflicts reaching at least 1,000 battle-related deaths. Because the data are in country-year format, we converted this information into war episodes based on the start and end dates of each conflict. This process generated 250 civil war episodes for our statistical analyses.

For our FID or intervention variable, we synthesized information from multiple datasets. We drew on prior RAND work to code information on 57 military interventions on the side of the government. Interventions on behalf of governments are defined as explicit military

[1] Peter Wallensteen and Margareta Sollenberg, "Armed Conflict 1989–2000," *Journal of Peace Research,* Vol. 38, No. 5, 2001.

support in the form of troops committed to combat in the conflict.[2] Accordingly, each intervention is coded by the maximum number of troops deployed during the conflict episode. As a minimum threshold, these interventions are limited to those with at least 100 "boots on the ground." Of these, 23 are U.S., seven are French, and four are British.[3] This approach excludes lesser forms of support, such as financing or military equipment. We also gathered information about interventions on behalf of rebels in these same 250 conflict episodes. For this purpose, we drew on the Non-State Actor (NSA) dataset, which includes information on whether a rebel group is supported by the government of a foreign state. Because we are interested in great-power competition, we limited our rebel support variable to reflect support from only the United States, Russia (Soviet Union), and China.[4] We defined support as any type of material support to the rebel group, including *military* (e.g., weapons or equipment) or *troops*.[5] Support to rebels is coded as a binary indicator. Russia/USSR supported rebels in ten cases, China supported rebels in eight, and the United States supported rebels in seven conflict episodes.

Modeling Approach

The outcomes of each conflict episode come from the political scientist Joakim Kreutz's conflict termination classification of the ACD.[6] These

---

2 Watts, Stephen, Patrick B. Johnston, Jennifer Kavanagh, Sean M. Zeigler, Bryan Frederick, Trevor Johnston, Karl P. Mueller, Astrid Stuth Cevallos, Nathan Chandler, Meagan L. Smith, Alexander Stephenson, and Julia A. Thompson, *Limited Intervention: Evaluating the Effectiveness of Limited Stabilization, Limited Strike, and Containment Operations*, Santa Monica, Calif.: RAND Corporation, RR-2037-A, 2017, p. 27.

3 See Watts et al., 2017, for more detail on sources and data collection for these interventions. They also include detailed information on intervention size for selected conflict episodes as well as force-to-population ratios.

4 We also included Iran and Cuba, but this had no impact on any reported outcomes.

5 The information came from the codebook and case description notes of Cunningham, Gleditsch, and Salehyan (2013b).

6 Kreutz, 2010.

outcomes include government victory, rebel victory, negotiated settlement, and "low activity."[7] Of the 250 conflicts identified in the UCDP dataset, 17 percent are classified as government victories, 9 percent are classified as rebel victories, 27 percent are identified as negotiated settlements, and 36 percent are identified as low-activity outcomes.

Because context is also an important factor in the success or failure of FID, our models control for several factors that should also affect conflict outcomes. These factors include the strength of rebel groups vis-à-vis the governments they face. As described above, external military support to rebel groups is also identified in each episode. We also control for the presence of peacekeepers, the length of the war, and insurgent goals (understood as either secessionist goals or the intent to seize control over the central government). Country-specific indicators include population size and regime type. We additionally include a Cold War indicator.[8]

As is well known, only the most pernicious and protracted of civil wars are likely to necessitate interventions by foreign governments. This implies a "selection effect," whereby states electing to support governments in civil wars do so only in the most difficult of circumstances, generally where rebel forces are the most capable. This creates difficulties for statistical estimations of the impact of interventions. To address this problem, we estimate our models in two steps or two successive models. The first stage of the model estimates which conflicts are likely to prompt military intervention on behalf of governments.[9] The results of this stage are used to generate a propensity score or weight for each conflict episode—an estimation of the probability of intervention in that war. These scores are then used to "weigh" the

---

7 For the purposes of our analysis, peace agreements have been combined with ceasefire outcomes and truces based upon Watts et al., 2017, consideration of the dataset.

8 Rebel strength is coded on a three-point scale: weaker or much weaker than the government (1), parity with the government (2), stronger or much stronger than the government (3). Peacekeeping is a binary measure. The length of each conflict episode is logged, as is population size. Regime type indicators come from Polity 2 scores. The interested reader can find more details in Watts et al., 2017.

9 This step is implemented through a logistic regression where *foreign intervention* is the outcome variable.

various observations in the second stage of the model.[10] This second stage estimates the effects of intervention (as well as the host of control variables) on the selected outcome variables (*government victory, rebel victory,* or *settlement*). [11]

Table A.1 reports the results of the first stage model (*intervention*). The estimated coefficients for each variable are listed in the table. The model controls for rebel strength, rebel support, Cold War, population (logged), peacekeeping operations, war type (control of government

Table A.1
Logistic Model of Pro-Government Intervention

Variable	Interventions
Rebel strength	0.532* (0.281)
Rebel support	0.565 (0.429)
Cold War	0.337 (0.426)
Population (logged)	0.399** (0.180)
Peacekeeping operations	2.267*** (0.591)
War type	2.300*** (0.536)
Oil barrels (logged)	–0.164*** (0.0520)
Constant	–13.21*** (3.542)
Observations	241
Log likelihood	–79.66
Pseudo R-squared	0.366

NOTES: Robust standard errors in parentheses.
*p < 0.1, **p < 0.05, ***p < 0.01.

[10] By this process, not all observations are equally assumed to receive the "treatment" or, in this case, intervention.

[11] For more details on this see Watts et al., 2017, pp. 35–37 and Appendix A.

versus separatist), and oil barrels produced on a yearly basis (logged). This is the first-stage model, used to generate all the (*outcome*) results noted in the report.

Table A.2 reports the results from several second-stage models on conflict outcomes, used to generate graphics in the report. Specifically, it includes the results for the following conflict outcomes: *government victory*, *negotiated settlement*, and either *government victory* or *negotiated settlement*. It also includes a categorical variable reflecting various troop

Table A.2
Logistic Models of Conflict Outcomes

Variable	Government Victory	Negotiated Settlement	Government Victory or Negotiated Settlement
100–2,000 troops	–1.782** (0.828)	2.359** (0.980)	0.880 (0.714)
2,001–5,000 troops	1.502** (0.738)	1.221 (o.809)	1.933*** (0.733)
More than 5,000 troops	1.557 (1.032)	1.241 (0.907)	1.957** (0.937)
Rebel strength	–0.074 (0.306)	–0.208 (0.341)	–0.149 (0.320)
Rebel support	–0.950** (0.434)	0.851 (0.747)	0.042 (0.494)
Cold War	1.127* (0.655)	–1.523*** (0.544)	–0.696 (0.447)
Peacekeeping operations	–1.803** (0.770)	1.743*** (0.685)	0.643 (0.640)
War type	0.769 (0.532)	–1.186* (0.685)	–0.470 (0.500)
Constant	–2.852*** (0.979)	0.959 (1.045)	0.992 (0.850)
Observations	212	212	212
Log likelihood	–141.9	–188.3	–227.9
Pseudo R-squared	0.162	0.201	0.096

NOTES: Robust standard errors clustered on conflict code in parentheses.

*p < 0.1, **p < 0.05, ***p < 0.01.

levels (if there was an intervention). The omitted troop category is *no troops*. Robust standard errors are clustered on the conflict identification code and reported in parentheses.

References

ACD—*See* UCDP/PRIO Armed Conflict Dataset, Uppsala Conflict Data Program at the Department of Peace and Conflict Research, Uppsala University, and the Centre for the Study of Civil War at the Peace Research Institute Oslo, version 4-2009, 2009; and Nils Petter Gleditsch, Peter Wallensteen, Mikael Eriksson, Margareta Sollenberg, and Håvard Strand, "Armed Conflict 1946–2001: A New Dataset," *Journal of Peace Research*, Vol. 39, No. 5, 2002, pp. 615–637.

Armstrong, Matthew, "No, We Do Not Need to Revive the U.S. Information Agency," *War on the Rocks*, November 12, 2015. As of October 25, 2019: https://warontherocks.com/2015/11/no-we-do-not-need-to-revive-the-u-s-information-agency/

Bab, Carla, "US Cuts Ties with Local Syrian Group Trained to Fight IS," *Voice of America*, July 27, 2017.

Bacevich, A. J., *American Military Policy in Small Wars: The Case of El Salvador*, Cambridge, Mass.: Institute for Foreign Policy Analysis, 1988.

Baldor, Lolita, "US General Visits Troops Fighting Islamic State in Syria," Associated Press, October 22, 2018.

Barnes, Julian E., "Cyber Command Operation Took Down Russian Troll Farm for Midterm Elections," *New York Times*, February 26, 2019.

Berinsky, Adam, "Rumors and Health Care Reform: Experiments in Political Misinformation," *British Journal of Political Science*, Vol. 47, No. 2, 2017.

Bernstein, Carl, "Cover Story: The Holy Alliance," *TIME*, June 24, 2001. As of October 12, 2019:
http://content.time.com/time/magazine/article/0,9171,159069,00.html

Blanton, Shannon Lindsey, "Foreign Policy in Transition? Human Rights, Democracy, and U.S. Arms Exports," *International Studies Quarterly*, Vol. 49, No. 4, December 2005, pp. 647–668.

Blechman, Barry M., and Stephen S. Kaplan, *Force Without War: United States Armed Forces as a Political Instrument*, Washington, D.C.: Brookings Institution Press, 1978.

Botti, David, "First Came ISIS, Then Iran: How the Mission at a U.S. Base in Syria Kept Growing," *New York Times,* February 4, 2019.

Bowman, Tom, "National Guard Plane 'Shoots' Message at Yugoslav Audience; U.S. Perspective on War, Rebuttal of Milosevic," *Baltimore Sun*, June 5, 1999.

Burton, Janice, "CMSE BiH," *Special Warfare Journal*, Vol., 29, No. 1, January–June 2016, pp. 18–20. As of October 12, 2019: https://www.soc.mil/SWCS/SWmag/archive/SW2901/Jan-June%20Special%20 Warfare2016.pdf

Childress, Michael, *The Effectiveness of U.S. Training Efforts in Internal Defense and Development: The Cases of El Salvador and Honduras*, Santa Monica, Calif.: RAND Corporation, MR-250-USDP, 1995. As of March 31, 2021: https://www.rand.org/pubs/monograph_reports/MR250.html

Cline, Lawrence E., "The U.S. Advisory Effort in El Salvador," in Kendall D. Gott and Michael G. Brooks, eds., *Security Assistance: U.S. and International Historical Perspectives: The Proceedings of the Combat Studies Institute 2006 Military History Symposium*, Fort Leavenworth, Kan.: Combat Studies Institute Press, 2006.

Congressional Research Service, *Army Security Force Assistance Brigades*, Washington, D.C., October 24, 2018.

Cunningham, David E., Kristian Skrede Gleditsch, and Idean Salehyan, "Non-State Actors in Civil Wars: A New Dataset," *Conflict Management and Peace Science*, Vol. 30, No. 5, 2013a, pp. 516–531.

Cunningham, David E., Kristian Skrede Gleditsch, and Idean Salehyan, Non-State Actor dataset, version 3.4, 2013b. As of March 31, 2021: http://ksgleditsch.com/eacd.html

DeVine, Michael, *Covert Action and Clandestine Activities of the Intelligence Community: Selected Definitions in Brief,* Washington, D.C.: Congressional Research Service, June 14, 2019.

Dobbins, James, Raphael S. Cohen, Nathan Chandler, Bryan Frederick, Edward Geist, Paul DeLuca, Forrest E. Morgan, Howard J. Shatz, and Brent Williams, *Extending Russia: Competing from Advantageous Ground*, Santa Monica, Calif.: RAND Corporation, RR-3063-A, 2019. As of March 31, 2021: https://www.rand.org/pubs/research_reports/RR3063.html

Driscoll, Jesse, and F. Daniel Hidalgo, "Intended and Unintended Consequences of Democracy Promotion Assistant to Georgia After the Rose Revolution," *Research and Politics*, Vol. 1, No. 1, 2014.

Ersan, Mohammed, "Syrian Rebel Commander: 150 US Troops at Al-Tanf Base," *Al-Monitor*, June 1, 2017.

Flanagan, Steven J., Jan Osburg, Anika Binnedijk, Marta Kepe, and Andrew Radin, *Deterring Russian Aggression in the Baltic States Through Resilience and Resistance*, Santa Monica, Calif.: RAND Corporation, RR-2779-OSD, 2019. As of March 21, 2021:
https://www.rand.org/pubs/research_reports/RR2779.html

Franz, Michael, and Travis Rideout, "Does Political Advertising Persuade?" *Political Behavior*, Vol. 29, No. 4, 2007.

Frederick, Bryan, Stephen Watts, Matthew Lane, Abby Doll, Ashley L. Rhoades, and Meagan L. Smith, *Understanding the Deterrent Impact of U.S. Overseas Forces*, Santa Monica, Calif.: RAND Corporation, RR-2533-A, 2018. As of March 31, 2021:
https://www.rand.org/pubs/research_reports/RR2533.html

Friedman, Herbert A., "PSYOP Against Milosevic's Yugoslavia," Psywar.org, January 1, 2007. As of October 12, 2019:
https://www.psywar.org/content/yugo

Geddes, Barbara, Joseph Wright, and Erica Frantz, "Autocratic Breakdown and Regime Transitions: A New Data Set," *Perspectives on Politics*, Vol. 12, No. 2, 2014, pp. 313–331.

Gerber, Alan, and Donald Green, "The Effects of Canvassing, Telephone Calls, and Direct Mail on Voter Turnout: A Field Experiment," *American Political Science Review*, Vol. 94, No. 3, 2000.

Gerber, Alan, Dan Green, and Christopher Larimer, "Social Pressure and Voter Turnout: Evidence from a Large-Scale Field Experiment," *American Political Science Review*, Vol. 102, No. 1, 2008.

Gleditsch, Nils Petter, Peter Wallensteen, Mikael Eriksson, Margareta Sollenberg, and Håvard Strand, "Armed Conflict 1946–2001: A New Dataset," *Journal of Peace Research*, Vol. 39, No. 5, 2002, pp. 615–637.

Haddick, Robert, *How Do SOF Contribute to Comprehensive Deterrence?* MacDill Air Force Base, Fla.: Joint Special Operations University Press, JSOU Report 17-11, 2017.

Huth, Paul K., "Deterrence and International Conflict: Empirical Findings and Theoretical Debates," *Annual Review of Political Science*, Vol. 2, 1999.

International Crisis Group, *Loose Ends: Iraq's Security Forces between U.S. Drawdown and Withdrawal*, Brussels, Belgium: ICG Middle East Report No. 99, October 2010.

Israel, Nick, and Albert Finochiarro, "6th MISB(A)'s Essential Role in the SOCEUR AOR," *Special Warfare Journal*, Vol. 29, No. 1, January–June 2016, pp. 71–73. As of October 12, 2019:
https://www.soc.mil/SWCS/SWmag/archive/SW2901/Jan-June%20Special%20Warfare2016.pdf

Jackson, Kimberly, "U.S. Special Operations Command," in S. Rebecca Zimmerman, Kimberly Jackson, Natasha Lander, Colin Roberts, Dan Madden, and Rebecca Orrie, *Movement and Maneuver: Culture and The Competition for Influence Among the U.S. Military Services*, Santa Monica, Calif.: RAND Corporation, RR-2270-OSD, 2019. As of March 31, 2021: https://www.rand.org/pubs/research_reports/RR2270.html

James, Brian W., "Sharpening the Spear of NATO SOF: Deterring Russian Hybrid Aggression Through Network Targeting," *Countering Terrorism Exchange*, Vol. 6, No. 4, 2016.

Jeong, Se-Hoon, Hyunyi Cho, and Yoori Hwang, "Media Literacy Interventions: A Meta-Analytic Review," *Journal of Communication*, Vol. 62, No. 3, 2012.

Johnson, David E., Karl P. Mueller, and William H. Taft, *Conventional Coercion Across the Spectrum of Operations: The Utility of U.S. Military Forces in the Emerging Security Environment*, Santa Monica, Calif.: RAND Corporation, MR-1494-A, 2003. As of March 31, 2021: https://www.rand.org/pubs/monograph_reports/MR1494.html

Joint Chiefs of Staff, *Special Operations*, Washington, D.C., Joint Publication 3-05, 2011.

Joint Chiefs of Staff, *Department of Defense Dictionary of Military and Associated Terms*, Washington, D.C., Joint Publication 1-02, February 15, 2016.

Joint Chiefs of Staff, *Joint Concept for Operating in the Information Environment*, Washington, D.C., July 25, 2018.

Joint Chiefs of Staff, *Competition Continuum*, Joint Doctrine Note 1-19, Washington, D.C., June 3, 2019.

Jones, Seth, *Waging Insurgent Warfare: Lessons from the Viet Cong to the Islamic State*, New York: Oxford University Press, 2017.

Jones, Seth, *A Covert Action: Reagan, the CIA, and the Cold War Struggle in Poland*, New York: W. W. Norton & Company, 2018.

Jones, Seth G., Andrew M. Liepman, and Nathan Chandler, *Counterterrorism and Counterinsurgency in Somalia: Assessing the Campaign Against Al Shabaab*, Santa Monica, Calif.: RAND Corporation, RR-1539-OSD, 2016. As of March 31, 2021: https://www.rand.org/pubs/research_reports/RR1539.html

Karim, Sabrina M., and William A. Wagstaff, "Keeping the Peace After Peacekeeping: How Peacekeepers Resolve the Security Dilemma in Post-Conflict States," unpublished paper, undated.

Kocher, Matthew Adam, Thomas B. Pepinsky, and Stathis N. Kalyvas, "Aerial Bombing and Counterinsurgency in the Vietnam War," *American Journal of Political Science*, Vol. 55, No. 2, April 2011, pp. 201–218.

Kreutz, Joakim, "How and When Armed Conflicts End: Introducing the UCDP Conflict Termination Dataset," *Journal of Peace Research*, Vol. 47, No. 2, 2010.

Ladwig, Walter C., "Influencing Clients in Counterinsurgency: U.S. Involvement in El Salvador's Civil War, 1979–92," *International Security*, Vol. 41, No. 1, Summer 2016.

"Largest Baltic Special Forces Exercise Flaming Sword 2015 Culminates in Combined Operation," *Baltic Times*, June 4, 2015. As of October 15, 2019: https://www.baltictimes.com/largest_baltic_special_forces_exercise_flaming_sword_2015_culminates_in_combined_operation/

Lau, Richard, Lee Sigelman, and Ivy Brown Rovner, "The Effects of Negative Political Campaigns: A Meta-Analytic Reassessment," *Journal of Politics*, Vol. 69, No. 4, 2007, pp. 1176–1209.

Long, Austin, Todd C. Helmus, S. Rebecca Zimmerman, Christopher M. Schnaubelt, and Peter Chalk, *Building Special Operations Partnerships in Afghanistan and Beyond: Challenges and Best Practices from Afghanistan, Iraq, and Colombia*, Santa Monica, Calif.: RAND Corporation, RR-713-OSD, 2015. As of March 31, 2021:
https://www.rand.org/pubs/research_reports/RR713.html

Maass, Peter, "3 U.S. Planes Begin Bosnian Relief Effort," *Washington Post*, March 1, 1993.

Madden, Dan, Dick Hoffmann, Michael Johnson, Fred Krawchuk, Bruce R. Nardulli, John E. Peters, Linda Robinson, and Abby Doll, *Toward Operational Art in Special Warfare*, Santa Monica, Calif.: RAND Corporation, RR-779-A, 2016, as of August 15, 2019:
https://www.rand.org/pubs/research_reports/RR779.html

Manwaring, Max G., and Court Prisk, "A Strategic View of Insurgencies: Insights from El Salvador," *Small Wars and Insurgencies*, Vol. 4, No. 1, Spring/Summer 1993.

McCulloch, Caitlin and Stephen Watts, *Evaluating the Effectiveness of Public Communication Campaigns and Their Implications for Strategic Competition with Russia*, Santa Monica, Calif.: RAND Corporation, RR-A412-2, 2021.

McNerney, Michael J., Angela O'Mahony, Thomas S. Szayna, Derek Eaton, Caroline Baxter, Colin P. Clarke, Emma Cutrufello, Michael McGee, Heather Peterson, Leslie Adrienne Payne, and Calin Trenkov-Wermuth, *Assessing Security Cooperation as a Preventive Tool*, Santa Monica, Calif.: RAND Corporation, RR-350-A, 2014. As of March 31, 2021:
https://www.rand.org/pubs/research_reports/RR350.html

Nickerson, David, Ryan Friedrichs, and David King, "Partisan Mobilization Campaigns in the Field: Results from a Statewide Turnout Experiment in Michigan," *Political Research Quarterly*, Vol. 59, No. 1, 2006.

NSA—*See* David E. Cunningham, Kristian Skrede Gleditsch, and Idean Salehyan, "Non-State Actors in Civil Wars: A New Dataset," *Conflict Management and Peace Science*, Vol. 30, No. 5, 2013a, pp. 516–531; and David E. Cunningham, Kristian Skrede Gleditsch, and Idean Salehyan, Non-State Actor dataset, version 3.4, 2013b.

Office of the Under Secretary of Defense (Comptroller), Chief Financial Officer, *Operation and Maintenance Overview, Fiscal Year 2018 Budget Estimates*, Washington, D.C.: U.S. Department of Defense, June 2017. As of October 26, 2019:
https://comptroller.defense.gov/Portals/45/Documents/defbudget/fy2018/fy2018_OM_Overview.pdf

Olson, Eric, "America's Not Ready for Today's Gray Wars," *Defense One*, December 10, 2015.

O'Rourke, Lindsey A., *Covert Regime Change: America's Secret Cold War*, Ithaca, N.Y.: Cornell University Press, 2018.

Park, Injoo, "Using PSYOP Against North Korea," Council on Foreign Relations, October 28, 2015, as of October 26, 2019:
https://www.cfr.org/blog/using-psyop-against-north-korea

Paterson, Patrick, *Training Surrogate Forces in International Humanitarian Law: Lessons from Peru, Colombia, El Salvador, and Iraq*, MacDill Air Force Base, Fla.: Joint Special Operations University Press, 2016.

Paul, Christopher, Colin P. Clarke, Beth Grill, Stephanie Young, Jennifer D. P. Moroney, Joe Hogler, and Christine Leah, *What Works Best When Building Partner Capacity and Under What Circumstances?* Santa Monica, Calif: RAND Corporation, MG-1253-OSD, 2013. As of March 31, 2021:
https://www.rand.org/pubs/monographs/MG1253z1.html

Paul, Christopher, and Miriam Matthews, *The Russian "Firehose of Falsehood" Propaganda Model*, Santa Monica, Calif: RAND Corporation, PE-198-OSD, 2016. As of March 31, 2021:
https://www.rand.org/pubs/perspectives/PE198.html

Peisakhin, Leonid, and Arturas Rozenas, "Electoral Effects of Biased Media: Russian Television in Ukraine," *American Journal of Political Science*, Vol. 62, No. 3, 2018.

Pillai, Chad M., "The Dark Arts: Application of Special Operations in Joint Strategic and Operational Plans," *Small Wars Journal*, June 7, 2018. As of August 8, 2018:
http://smallwarsjournal.com/jrnl/art/dark-arts-application-special-operations-joint-strategic-and-operational-plans

Powelson, Simon J., "Enduring Engagement Yes, Episodic Engagement No: Lessons for SOF from Mali," master's thesis, Monterey, Calif.: Naval Postgraduate School, December 2013.

Public Law 116-92, National Defense Authorization Act for Fiscal Year 2020, December 20, 2019.

Rouse, Ed, "Psychological Operations & Operation Allied Forces," Psywarrior.com, undated. As of October 12, 2019:
http://www.psywarrior.com/kosovo.html

Quinlivan, James T., "Coup-Proofing: Its Practice and Consequences in the Middle East," *International Security*, Vol. 24, No. 2, Fall 1999, pp. 131–165.

Radio Free Europe/Radio Liberty, "About Us," undated. As of October 25, 2019:
https://pressroom.rferl.org/about-us

Ramasubramanian, Srividya, "Media-Based Strategies to Reduce Racial Stereotypes Activated by News Stories," *Journalism and Mass Communication Quarterly*, Vol. 84, No. 2, 2007.

Rasmussen, Sune Engel, and Michael R. Gordon, "A Small U.S. Base Gets in Iran's Way—But Maybe Not for Long," *Wall Street Journal*, December 27, 2018.

Robinson, Linda, Patrick B. Johnston, and Gillian S. Oak, *U.S. Special Operations Forces in the Philippines, 2001–2014*, Santa Monica, Calif.: RAND Corporation, RR-1236-OSD, 2016. As of March 31, 2021:
https://www.rand.org/pubs/research_reports/RR1236.html

Ruby, Tomislav Z., and Douglas Gibler, "US Professional Military Education and Democratization Abroad," *European Journal of International Relations*, Vol. 16, No. 3, 2010.

"Saber Junction 2018 Integrated NATO, Partner SOF with Conventional Forces," *Army Recognition*, October 30, 2018. As of October 15, 2019:
https://www.armyrecognition.com/analysis_focus_army_defence_military_industry_army/saber_junction_2018_integrated_nato_partner_sof_with_conventional_forces.html

Savage, Jesse Dillon, and Jonathan Caverley, "When Human Capital Threatens the Capitol: Foreign Aid in the Form of Military Training and Coups," *Journal of Peace Research*, Vol. 54, No. 4, 2017.

Schweller, Randall L., "Tripolarity and the Second World War," *International Studies Quarterly*, Vol. 37, No. 1, 1993.

South, Todd, "Cyber Skills Needed: Special Ops Leaders Seek Soldiers Who Can Fight the Enemy Up Close and Online," *Army Times*, October 3, 2017. As of October 12, 2019:
https://www.armytimes.com/news/your-army/2017/10/03/hackers-wanted-special-ops-leaders-seek-soldiers-who-can-fight-the-enemy-up-close-and-online/

Taylor, Guy, "State Department Global Engagement Center Targets Russian Propaganda, 'Deep Fakes,'" Associated Press, December 12, 2018.

Toft, Monica Duffy and Yuri M. Zhukov, "Denial and Punishment in the North Caucasus: Evaluating the Effectiveness of Coercive Counterinsurgency," *Journal of Peace Research*, Vol. 49, No. 6, 2012, pp. 785–800.

TRADOC—*See* U.S. Army Training and Doctrine Command.

Tucker, David and Christopher J. Lamb, *United States Special Operations Forces*, New York: Columbia University Press, 2007.

Tully, Melissa, Emily Vraga, and Leticia Bode, "Designing and Testing News Literacy Messages for Social Media," *Mass Communication and Society*, Vol. 23, No. 1, 2020.

UCDP/PRIO Armed Conflict Dataset, Uppsala Conflict Data Program at the Department of Peace and Conflict Research, Uppsala University, and the Centre for the Study of Civil War at the Peace Research Institute Oslo, version 4-2009, 2009. As of March 31, 2021:
https://www.prio.org/Data/Armed-Conflict/UCDP-PRIO/

United States of America v. Internet Research Agency LLC et al., 18 U.S.C. §§ 2, 371, 1349, 10281A. As of March 31, 2021:
https://assets.documentcloud.org/documents/4380504/The-Special-Counsel-s-Indictment-of-the-Internet.pdf

U.S. Advisory Commission on Public Diplomacy, *2018 Comprehensive Annual Report on Public Diplomacy and International Broadcasting*, Washington, D.C.: U.S. Department of State, 2019.

U.S. Army Training and Doctrine Command, *The U.S. Army in Multi-Domain Operations 2028,* Fort Eustis, Va., TRADOC Pamphlet 525-3-1, December 6, 2018.

U.S. Senate, Committee on Appropriations, *Department of State, Foreign Operations, and Related Programs Appropriations Bill, 2019, Report 115-282*, Washington, D.C.: U.S. Government Printing Office, 2018.

U.S. Department of Defense, *Summary of the National Defense Strategy of the United States of America: Sharpening the American Military's Competitive Edge*, Washington, D.C., 2018.

U.S. Special Operations Command, *United States Special Operations Command Comprehensive Review*, January 23, 2020. As of March 31, 2021:
https://sof.news/ussocom/ussocom-sof-culture-ethics-report-2020/

Votel, Joseph L., Charles T. Cleveland, Charles T. Connett, and Will Irwin, "Unconventional Warfare in the Gray Zone," *Joint Force Quarterly*, Vol. 80, 1st Quarter 2016, pp. 101–109.

Vraga, Emily, and Melissa Tully, "Media Literacy Messages and Hostile Media Perceptions: Processing of Nonpartisan Versus Partisan Political Information," *Mass Communication and Society*, Vol. 15, No. 4, 2015.

Waghelstein, John D., *Military-to-Military Contacts: Personal Observations—The El Salvador Case*, unpublished draft, Newport, R.I.: U.S. Naval War College, 2002.

Wallensteen, Peter, and Margareta Sollenberg, "Armed Conflict 1989–2000," *Journal of Peace Research*, Vol. 38, No. 5, 2001.

Wasser, Becca, Ben Connable, Anthony Atler, and James Sladden, eds., *Comprehensive Deterrence Forum: Proceedings and Commissioned Papers*, Santa Monica, Calif.: RAND Corporation, CF-345-A, 2018. As of March 31, 2021: https://www.rand.org/pubs/conf_proceedings/CF345.html

Watts, Stephen, *Identifying and Mitigating Risks in Security Sector Assistance for Africa's Fragile States*, Santa Monica, Calif.: RAND Corporation, RR-808-A, 2015. As of March 31, 2021: https://www.rand.org/pubs/research_reports/RR808.html

Watts, Stephen, Patrick B. Johnston, Jennifer Kavanagh, Sean M. Zeigler, Bryan Frederick, Trevor Johnston, Karl P. Mueller, Astrid Stuth Cevallos, Nathan Chandler, Meagan L. Smith, Alexander Stephenson, and Julia A. Thompson, *Limited Intervention: Evaluating the Effectiveness of Limited Stabilization, Limited Strike, and Containment Operations*, Santa Monica, Calif.: RAND Corporation, RR-2037-A, 2017. As of March 31, 2021: https://www.rand.org/pubs/research_reports/RR2037.html

Watts, Stephen, Trevor Johnston, Matthew Lane, Sean Mann, Michael J. McNerney, and Andrew Brooks, *Building Security in Africa: An Evaluation of U.S. Security Sector Assistance in Africa from the Cold War to the Present*, Santa Monica, Calif.: RAND Corporation, RR-2447-OSD, 2018. As of March 31, 2021: https://www.rand.org/pubs/research_reports/RR2447.html

Weisman, Michael, "NATO, Partner Spec Ops Forces Rapidly Deploy for Trojan Footprint 18," Air National Guard website, June 12, 2018. As of October 15, 2019: https://www.ang.af.mil/Media/Article-Display/Article/1548092/nato-partner-spec-ops-forces-rapidly-deploy-for-trojan-footprint-18/

The White House, *National Security Strategy of the United States of America*, Washington, D.C., December 2017.

White-Jenkins, Tatyana, "Exercise Hedgehog," *Citizen-Soldier*, October 5, 2018. As of October 15, 2019: https://citizen-soldiermagazine.com/exercise-hedgehog/

Williams, Lauren C., "2020 Budget Boosts Funding for Cyber Forces, AI," *Defense Systems*, March 11, 2019.

Witty, David, *The Iraqi Counter Terrorism Service*, Washington, D.C.: Brookings Institution, 2014.

Zeigler, Sean M., Dara Massicot, Elina Treyger, Naoko Aoki, Chandler Sachs, and Stephen Watts, *Analysis of Russian Irregular Threats*, Santa Monica, Calif.: RAND Corporation, RR-A412-3, 2021.